ADELPHI
Paper • 296

The Crisis of the Iranian State

Contents

Oxford University Press, Walton Street, Oxford OX2 6DP
Oxford New York
Athens Auckland Bangkok Bombay
Calcutta Cape Town Dar es Salaam Delhi
Florence Hong Kong Istanbul Karachi
Kuala Lumpur Madras Madrid Melbourne
Mexico City Nairobi Paris Singapore
Taipei Tokyo Toronto
and associated companies in
Berlin Ibadan

Oxford is a trade mark of Oxford University Press

Published in the United States
by Oxford University Press Inc., New York

© The International Institute for Strategic Studies 1995

First published July 1995 by Oxford University Press for
The International Institute for Strategic Studies
23 Tavistock Street, London WC2E 7NQ

Director: Dr John Chipman
Assistant Editor: Juliet Sampson

British Library Cataloguing in Publication Data

Data available

Library of Congress Cataloging in Publication Data

ISBN 0-19-828023-8
ISSN 0567-932X

INTRODUCTION

The Islamic Republic of Iran is facing an existential crisis. It is ideologically bankrupt, economically and morally exhausted, militarily weak, increasingly unpopular domestically, and isolated and friendless abroad. In February 1994, as the clerics celebrated their fifteenth year in power, a bizarre assassination attempt against President Ali Akbar Hashemi Rafsanjani and the outbreak of Sunni riots in the south-eastern city of Zahedan further damaged the regime's confidence. The Iranian new year (*Nouruz*) celebrations in March 1994 were tense; bombs exploded, and the crowd clashed with security forces. Disturbances continued to plague the government throughout the summer of 1994, with rioting and demonstrations in Najafabad, Qazvin and Tabriz. On two separate occasions, senior officers of the armed forces warned the mullahs of impending catastrophe and called upon them to step down in the interest of the Iranian nation. During the winter of 1994–95, Iran's economic situation deteriorated following a dramatic drop in the value of the currency, the rial, against major international currencies.

Iran's weaknesses and internal turmoil are beginning to elicit more commentary from the outside world.[1] Nonetheless, the prevailing consensus in the West and the Middle East is that Iran is a menace to regional stability and Western interests. Attention continues to focus on Iran's propensity for mischief-making, deep-seated ideological differences with its neighbours, hegemonic aspirations in the Persian Gulf, and its rearmament programme, including its quest for nuclear weapons.[2] Tehran's vocal opposition to the Arab–Israeli peace process, and Western suspicion that Iran was involved in terrorist attacks against Israeli and Jewish targets in London, Buenos Aires and Panama in the summer of 1994 have given weight to the view that Iran is a threat.

This study takes into consideration the arguments of the prevailing orthodoxy about Iran and goes beyond it. Instead of focusing on Iran as a source of threat, it looks at the hazards and severe problems currently facing the rulers of Iran. This paper argues that the Islamic Republic faces a variety of acute pressures and threats to its political legitimacy, domestic stability and national security. The Islamic Republic no longer has the political, economic or ideological means to achieve the goals it has set for itself.

These goals included the creation of a modern and strong centralised state administering an independent and dynamic economy; a nation free of foreign political and economic domination or interference, culturally independent, regionally influential and equipped with powerful armed forces. The Islamic rulers share these goals with their predecessors, the Pahlavis. Both groups resented and attempted to transcend Iran's decline.

Mohammed Reza Shah was convinced that it was his destiny to lead Iran into modernity, or *tamaddon-e-bozorg* (the Great Civilisation). He consolidated his power and allied himself with the United States. In 1977, on the eve of the Revolution, imperial Iran was at the height of its prestige and power. Yet the Pahlavis failed in their efforts to transform Iran. Despite modernisation, inflation and unemployment were high and the standard of living was falling. The vast majority of Iranians did not share their monarch's view that Iran was prosperous, modern and respected. They resented the large US presence in their country and the Shah's superficial Westernisation policies implemented by a 'Westoxified' elite. Anger was directed at the misuse of oil revenues, widespread repression, pervasive political corruption, and wasteful expenditure on a large technologically advanced military that was dependent on the United States.

The Iranian Revolution was a collective rejection of the Pahlavi modernisation programme and of Western, particularly American, influence. The religious establishment under the charismatic leadership of Ayatollah Khomeini was the best organised and most articulate of the opposition groups. This enabled it to seize control of the post-Revolutionary state and consolidate its power. But attempts to implement far-reaching political and socio-economic programmes in the first ten years of the Islamic Republic – the period between 1979–89, known as the 'first republic' – succumbed to intense factional strife and an obsessive focus on the war with Iraq that raged from 1980–88.

Iran's defeat in the war with Iraq represented a comprehensive defeat of the 'radical' phase; Ayatollah Khomeini himself declared how painful it had been to drink from the 'poisoned chalice' of the cease-fire. His death in June 1989 was a turning-point in the political history of the Islamic Republic. Khomeini left his faithful lieutenants a host of unresolved problems. These included a cacophony of conflicting views on the future direction of a devastated economy and scarred society; structural weaknesses in and controversy over the nature of the political system; and a highly politicised clerical establishment whose legitimacy had declined precipitously in the course of a decade.

After Khomeini's death, a period of intense reassessment of the achievements and failures of the first decade took place. Following the reassessment, a coalition of pragmatic clerics and technocrats headed by President and former *Majlis ash-Shoura* (Consultative Council) speaker Rafsanjani established what has come to be known as the 'second republic'.[3] The coalition attempted to strengthen the powers of the central state, rebuild Iran's defences, implement a programme of economic reconstruction and reform, and undertake an opening to the outside world – without which the new domestic agenda would not succeed.

Now, in the mid-1990s, the forces of change in the second republic are in retreat, having come into conflict with the Islamic Republic as an entrenched system. This is not as paradoxical as it sounds. The 'second republic' intended to transcend the vagaries, vested interests, severe factionalism, and bureaucratic inefficiencies associated with the Islamic Republic in order to implement far-reaching economic reforms. But it has not been successful; reforms were implemented half-heartedly or faced tremendous institutional and political obstacles. High post-war popular expectations have not been met; discontent and alienation are growing.

The Islamic Republic has been shaken by a severe crisis of political legitimacy that is eroding the foundations of the system established by Ayatollah Khomeini. His successor, Ayatollah Khamene'i, has neither Khomeini's charisma nor his spiritual and religious qualifications. Blatant abuse of power and rampant corruption by the political clergy has further eroded the second republic's legitimacy.

There is growing instability in peripheral regions with large refugee populations, porous borders and unstable neighbours. But the potentially most serious regional problem is the ethno-sectarian dispute between the Sunni populations and the Shi'i Iranian state.

Iran's foreign policy continues to defy easy categorisation. In the first decade of its existence, the Islamic Republic of Iran was unequivocally a revolutionary state opposed to the regional status quo and domination of the world by the two superpowers; it followed the pattern of revolutionary states that have destabilised the international system to bring about change in the conduct of inter-state relations and domestic politics in other states.[4]

After the war with Iraq, the political elite recognised that militant confrontation with the outside world had been counterproductive. As a result, economic reform and reconstruction in the second republic depended on adopting a policy of openness towards the outside world. This meant Iran had to improve relations with the West, a fact President Rafsanjani and his group of Western-educated technocrats has clearly recognised. But the Islamic Republic's turbulent relations with the Western world indicate that an element of schizophrenia pervades Iran's international behaviour in the 1990s. Iran has not been able to bridge the gap between the logic of state interests and Revolutionary policies in any consistent manner.

Incoherence is also starkly evident in Iran's defence policies. The armed forces and defence industries are a microcosm of the inefficient, factionalised and ramshackle state they serve. For the past two centuries, most of Iran's rulers have been engaged in an unsuccessful quest to create effective national armed forces. Between the 1920s and the 1970s, Iran's armed forces suffered 3,000 casualties, 90% against internal insurgents. In the first two weeks of the Iran–Iraq War, the Iranians suffered 33,000 casualties against an external enemy.[5] In the course of the war, a modern national military tradition was finally born; but military effectiveness still eludes the rulers of Iran.

Iran's military revitalisation programme has run into difficulties. It lacks adequate financial resources and a diversity of suppliers to equip conventional forces with large quantities of qualitatively advanced weapons. It faces severe problems in streamlining and rationalising the military structure. Defence industries are poorly organised, technologically backward and lack the necessary skilled technical cadre. If Iran's strategy to rebuild its conventional forces is ultimately unsuccessful, it may concentrate its efforts on developing or acquiring weapons of mass destruction (WMD) in the belief that they are a cheap and efficient deterrent and retaliatory capability.

This study explains the origins and implications for the Islamic Republic of the severe crises it is undergoing, explores the directions the Islamic Republic is likely to take in the second half of the 1990s. Whatever its long-term future may be, the Islamic Republic's short- and medium-term prospects are grim.

I. THE DOMESTIC CONTEXT OF SECURITY

The salient feature of the Islamic Republic of Iran 16 years after the 1979 Revolution remains the growing gap between the regime's ideological rhetoric and the population's material needs, which have still not been met. Since its inception in 1979 the Islamic Republic has gone from failure to failure, falling far short of the dreams of its founders and supporters. Its people have emerged from ten years of war and revolution discontented and exhausted, looking to the government to provide the rewards it had promised. Iran has not yet implemented these promises of social justice and economic development. The Islamic Republic now exists not as a 'serene puritanical society', but rather as a chaotic and morally hypocritical society characterised by massive corruption, influence-peddling, an extensive black-market economy, crime and high inflation.[1] Six years on, the Islamic Republic has failed to shake off the dismal legacy of its first decade.

The Legacy of the First Republic
The first republic's failure to implement economic development and social justice programmes stemmed from its inability to formulate either consistent or rational public policies.[2] Revolutions are, by nature, disruptive events that take a long time to dissipate. The ongoing war with Iraq and Iran's international isolation preoccupied the new regime. But the real reason for this policy failure was the deep-seated inter-clerical factionalism regarding the direction of the economy and of society. The inability to resolve fundamental factional disputes led to a paralysis of decision-making.[3] Though they tried to present a united front, state officials acknowledged that profound policy differences existed within the vast political-clerical establishment that professed fealty to Ayatollah Khomeini and the Islamic Republic.[4]

The clergy's radical or hardline faction, generally made up of younger, more militant clerics from poor backgrounds, was buoyed by mass Revolutionary hysteria and Khomeini's support for him in the 1980s. It targeted for destruction the capitalist development characteristic of the Pahlavi period. The radicals' underlying principles were to be economically self-sufficient and independent, diversify the economy away from oil, and satisfy the social needs of the population, particularly the less privileged members of society for whom the Revolution had been waged. Socio-economic and social welfare reforms were motivated by a genuine desire to help the

7

dispossessed and reduce the large social disparities between rich and poor. Arguing that the Koran sanctioned a socialistic approach, the radicals insisted that the Islamic Republic provide basic needs such as housing, food, health care, decent labour laws, free education, land reform and a social safety net for those on low or fixed incomes.

The radicals' economic strategy included nationalising enterprises and curbing the size of private property. They forcibly expropriated a wide range of private enterprises belonging to members of the upper classes and the bourgeoisie who were linked to the *ancien régime*. These businesses were placed under the control of parastatal Revolutionary foundations – the *bonyads* – which were founded ostensibly as charitable institutions to provide for the needs of the dispossessed. The state took control of a wide range of economic activities, including the exchange rate, while the private sector was given a secondary and residual economic role. There was nothing specifically Islamic about this strategy, which had more in common with socialist and Marxist economic visions that several other Third World states had adopted in the past.

Support for the radical agenda came from the lower classes or, in the terminology of the Islamic Republic, the downtrodden oppressed masses (*musta'zafin*) of the urban slums. The Iranian equivalent of the *pieds-nus* or *sans-culottes* of the French Revolution, the political power of this social class was best exemplified by the *hizbollahi*, a young, bearded, angry man recruited from the poorest sectors of society. Described as one who 'does not use *eau de cologne*, wear a tie or smoke American cigarettes', the *hizbollahi* represented the austere and puritanical face of Revolutionary Islam.[5]

Opposition to the regime comprised a large and influential group of conservative clerics who used the Koran to argue that Islam sanctioned capitalism in Islamic society. The poor understanding of the Islamic approach to economics and the fact that Islam was open to interpretation often enabled the conservative and rightist clergy to attack the radicals' strategy on the grounds that it was incompatible with Islamic precepts. The conservatives stood for the sanctity of private property and greater freedom for private enterprise. They wanted minimal government interference in the economy and an economic policy more open to the outside world. For them, capitalism was based on speculation, trade and commerce, and they believed that indigenous Islamic culture should be the bulwark of this Islamic capitalist system. Hence, they have been described as 'economically liberal but culturally hardline conservatives', or alternatively, as the embodiment of the 'unity of the market and of the *chador*' (modest Islamic dress).[6] Socially, the conservative clerics represented traditional monied interests: wealthy *bazaaris* who had amassed their fortune in trading, commerce and speculation; and landlords who feared land reform.

The middle ground of the political spectrum was occupied by a group of technocrats and pragmatic clerics who did not constitute a religious-political bloc with a coherent ideologically based vision of society. Pragmatism, the hallmark of the technocrats and certain clerics, like Rafsanjani, emerged as a policy position in the course of the 1980s when these individuals became aware of, and disenchanted with, Iran's self-destructive course in socio-economic affairs, the war with Iraq, and Iran's international diplomacy. The technocrats did not represent a social class. Unlike the radicals – many of whom amassed fortunes – who do not represent a property-owning class, or the conservatives who do, the technocrats have always merely managed national wealth in the interests of the state and society as a whole.[7]

Despite his uncontested supreme religious and political authority, Ayatollah Khomeini did not take sides in the struggle between the two clerical factions over the direction of Iran's society and economy. He was clearly sympathetic to the socio-economic agenda of the radicals because it was directed towards improving the lot of the dispossessed. As he once said: 'We must make all efforts to serve the *musta'zafin* who has been oppressed throughout history, and the government should always give priority to him'.[8] The downtrodden were the bedrock of the Revolution and represented the raw political power that brought down the Pahlavis and, in the course of the war with Iraq, provided the multitude of fervent individuals seeking martyrdom who then died by the thousands in the war. The Revolution had to attend to them and their families; losing their support would have been fatal to the stability and legitimacy of the regime. But, shrewd politician that he was, Ayatollah Khomeini knew that the Islamic Republic could not afford to alienate the conservative clerics and the wealthy *bazaaris*. He allowed the extremely conservative Council of Guardians to veto important social legislation that it believed conflicted with sacred law and violated the sanctity of private property. Yet Khomeini would not allow either group to go too far because ultimately the survival of the Islamic Revolution mattered most. The paralysis that emerged from this delicate balance between social forces guaranteed its survival.

The Domestic Impact of the Iran–Iraq War
The other central preoccupation of the regime was the bloody war with Iraq that dominated everyday life. Iran's Supreme Leader, Ayatollah Ali Khamene'i, became the incarnation of a society that saw itself as having been unjustly attacked by outside powers. The war helped the clerics consolidate their power against their internal enemies and enabled the radical faction to increase its control over the economy. Ultimately, the war became the excuse for the lack of economic and social progress. Winning the war became the yardstick with which to measure the success of the Islamic Republic.

But even in the war, Iran failed dismally. After 1982 when it went on the offensive, the war transformed an already inefficient Third World command economy into an equally inefficient wartime economy with subsidies, rationing and price controls that nevertheless failed to sustain Iran's war effort. By 1988, the war with Iraq was absorbing 40–50% of state revenues leaving little for the needs of the population. Large fluctuations in oil prices in the mid-1980s, compounded by Iraqi attacks on the oil-producing infrastructure, were calamitous for a country dependent on oil revenues.

The Political and Economic Agenda of the Second Republic
Once the war with Iraq ended the Iranian regime no longer had an excuse for its lack of progress towards a just society. The Islamic Republic was faced with the distortions and upheavals caused by its Revolutionary policies and the massive destruction caused by the war, including a severely battered economic and industrial infrastructure, rampant inflation, unemployment and underemployment, a huge gap between the rich and the poor, and pervasive corruption. The nationalised industries, operating at between 10–30% of total capacity, were unproductive. The bureaucracy had doubled in size, but was corrupt, inefficient and unresponsive to people's needs. The subsidy system was marred by corruption and poor distribution. The result was a spiralling rise in basic goods prices putting them out of reach of the urban poor. Per capita income was halved between 1979 and 1989. After ten years of hardship, austerity and war Iran's population welcomed change.

This was a state of affairs that a group of pragmatic clerics like *Majlis* Speaker Rafsanjani, President Ali Khamene'i and Western-educated technocrats sought to change. Rafsanjani and Khamene'i spent the year between the acceptance of the July 1988 cease-fire with Iraq and Ayatollah Khomeini's death in June 1989 implementing a multi-pronged strategy to divest the radicals of their stranglehold on power by attacking them politically, deriding their ideological message, and eroding their institutional power base. The strategy accelerated once Rafsanjani was elected President in 1989 and Khamene'i became Supreme Leader. The hardliners were out-manoeuvred in the political process by the *de facto* alliance that emerged in 1989 between Rafsanjani and the technocrats, on the one hand, and the conservatives, on the other.

The rulers of the second republic believed that the radicals' *modus operandi* had been catastrophic for Iran. It had been a decade of extremism, irrationality, ideological sloganeering and deception. In contrast, Rafsanjani pleaded for a rational approach to economic matters. There had been no long-term strategic planning, either with respect to the economy or the war. Revolutionary turmoil and hubris could not continue forever. Those on the right and centre attacked as erroneous and misguided the radicals' ideal of an Islam that promoted hardship, poverty, simplicity, ignorance and austerity. Following his accession to the presidency in 1989, Rafsanjani stated that such qualities are not virtues.[9] The radicals were attacked for their hypocrisy in preaching a simple and austere Islam for the people, while enriching themselves.

Ayatollah Khomeini's death represented more than the end of the 'first republic'. With his disappearance the radicals lost a sympathetic voice and a key protector in the internal balance of power between the two key clerical factions.[10]

Constitutional reforms implemented in summer 1989 were intended to rid the 1979 Constitution of the structural inconsistencies created by a dual-nature executive in which the President had shared executive powers with the Prime Minister. This had created friction between the posts, particularly over the implementation of socio-economic reforms and the nomination of ministers. This method of power-sharing could not continue in the post-war era. The Islamic Republic could either have a parliamentary-style executive with a prime minister, or it could establish a strong presidential-style executive. The constitutional review committee opted for the latter. The President, who had formerly played a largely ceremonial role, was given a strong policy-making role. This presidential system was not welcomed by the radicals because it would weaken the *Majlis*, where even at the end of the 1980s they remained powerfully ensconced. In July 1989, Rafsanjani won the presidential elections with an overwhelming majority of the popular vote. The vote was a message to the clerics that the people wanted profound change, and a strengthened presidency would be the instrument to bring it about.

Radicals were purged from many state institutions and replaced by men committed to non-ideological reforms and efficiency. Despite pressure from the *Majlis*, Rafsanjani refused to include some well-known radical clerics in his first cabinet. The cabinet consisted almost entirely of Western-educated technocrats (so-called 'PhDs with beards') like Mohsen Nourbaksh and Mohammed Adeli – who became Minister of Economics and Finance, and Governor of the Central Bank, respectively. Men like these not only reiterated their view that economics was incompatible with ideology, but barely concealed their admiration for the increasingly dynamic Asian economies.

Both the pragmatists and conservatives joined forces in October 1990 to exclude radical candidates from participating in elections to the Assembly of Experts, the body that elects the *faqih*, the Supreme Leader. Excluding them from that Assembly was intended to remove those who might have made life difficult for Khomeini's successor as *faqih*, Ayatollah Khamene'i.

The weakening of the radicals set the stage for the smooth implementation of the strategy of reconstruction. The strategy included several integrated elements: economic reconstruction and development; economic reform of a highly distorted economy; and an economic opening to the outside world.

The exact financial cost to Iran of the war with Iraq has been a source of controversy generating considerable debate. President Rafsanjani claimed in late August 1994 that Iran had suffered damages of one trillion dollars.[11] The second republic faced the awesome task of repairing the damage suffered by urban areas in the war zone and the industrial infrastructure, especially oil and petrochemical. Reconstructing these revenue-generating industries was a top priority; bringing them to nearly full capacity was done with uncharacteristic speed and efficiency.

The economic liberalism of the technocrats and conservatives implied a clear-cut rejection of the political economy of the radicals. The state would continue to control some key industries, including strategic ones. But the technocrats' economic liberalism would mean a thorough abandonment of the rigid *étatisme* of the previous ten years. In its place the government preached the virtues of shock-therapy reform as advocated by the International Monetary Fund and the World Bank with which the technocrats restored links. In brief, the technocrats advocated: privatisation of inefficient state enterprises; removal of price controls; elimination of the system of subsidies; and unification of the anarchic system of multiple exchange rates. They wished to expunge the factors that had caused massive distortions in the economy and contributed to the decline in the standard of living of all social strata. Rafsanjani's reconstruction programme was enshrined in the first Five Year Plan of 1990–94. For the pragmatists and technocrats, implementing reforms and reversing the policies of the first decade would ensure not only the survival of the Islamic Republic, but enable it to implement the dream of a model Islamic society worthy of emulation by other Islamic societies.

The Economic and Social Failures of the Second Republic
By late 1994, President Rafsanjani's economic reform programmes were clearly in disarray. There were economic, social and political contradictions within the reforms themselves. And reform is not merely a technical process, which in the case of the Islamic Republic would have been implemented by a highly capable and motivated technocratic cadre supported by the political system. Reform inevitably brings in its wake profound changes in the allocation of resources, status and power. As a result, reform faced resistance from groups with veto power, many of whom had vested interests – whether material or ideological – threatened by change. The Iranian radicals challenged reform because their political legitimacy would be questioned if reform were to destroy the present system.

Internal Contradictions of the Reform Process
One of the greatest structural economic problems that Iran has faced is its overwhelming dependence on oil-export revenue – 85–90% of its total revenue. The Islamic Republic's goal was a long-term strategy to reduce this chronic dependence on oil revenue. Yet at the same time it sought to ensure that oil quotas within the Organisation of Petroleum-Exporting Countries (OPEC) were maintained to keep oil prices, and thus revenues, high in order to finance its war with Iraq and, after 1989, its economic development plans. Iran is still, in the 1990s, highly dependent on oil revenue. Consequently, its budget remains subject to the volatile fluctuations of the oil market. While the oil slump of 1986 seriously affected Iran's ability to wage war with Iraq, the sudden jump in oil prices in 1990–91 following the Kuwait crisis netted Iran income of $18 billion. The subsequent drop in oil prices has had a catastrophic effect on economic reconstruction programmes. In 1992–93 Iran earned $16bn in oil-export revenue, while in 1994 it barely made $12bn. Compounding its falling income is the decline in the productive capa-

bilities of its major oilfields, poor maintenance of equipment and lack of sufficient technical and managerial expertise, all of which have hindered Iran's ability to reach its maximum production capability of 4.2m barrels per day.[12] Such fluctuations and structural weaknesses within the oil industry has made it very difficult for the President and the technocrats consistently to implement economic reconstruction plans. The technocrats were overly optimistic in their belief that oil revenue would average over $20bn annually during the first Five Year Plan, which called for hard-currency expenditures of $112bn.

Foreign borrowing proved to be controversial. Iran emerged from the war with Iraq with virtually no debt problem, unlike Iraq. The Islamic Republic's prompt payments and efficient management of its external finances ensured the country's impressive credit rating. This concern with being debt-free was primarily ideological: the radicals wanted Iran to avoid ties to the Western-dominated international financial markets. But from 1989 onwards, it became clear that the economic reconstruction and recovery programme required access to Western capital. The government did not have any significant budget surplus and private investors in Iran were reluctant to invest in productive enterprises, preferring to put their money into dormant savings or property speculation.

In order to maintain a political consensus the government eschewed long-term debt obligations – the Western states were also reluctant to lend to Iran on a long-term basis – and settled on short-term loans to finance its recovery programme. But the government then found itself in serious trouble. The sudden surge in oil prices following Iraq's invasion of Kuwait in August 1990 – caused first by the panic that the invasion occasioned, and then by the subsequent disappearance of both Iraq and Kuwait from the oil market – tempted the Iranian government into a spending spree. The Central Bank lost control over the number of letters-of-credit issued by commercial banks in Iran. In 1992, letters-of-credit payments on short-term debts fell behind schedule for the first time since the Revolution, severely damaging Iran's credit rating. The government's inability to control spending caused a severe debt crisis by 1993, with the country acknowledging short-term debts of $30–$40bn. By early 1994 the country was $10bn in arrears to its Western creditors. This crisis has had a ripple effect on the rest of the economy.

The government squeezed expenditure, slowing the high growth rate achieved in 1990–91 and forcing a sharp reduction in imports.

The high growth rates had fuelled an import spree filling shops with spare parts, raw materials for industry and consumer goods that the Iranian public had not seen for a decade. But imports have fallen; not only consumer goods, but basic commodities and spare parts are again scarce, dashing expectations of a brighter future. The fact that Iran has been forced to cut imports since 1992 – imports fell by 50% in 1994 – has deprived its industries of raw materials and spare parts, and forced many state industries to freeze wages or to close, causing thousands of lay-offs.

The essential elements of Iran's economic reform programme were to rationalise the world's most convoluted multi-exchange-rate system, encourage private investment and the return of skilled expatriates, and lower subsidics. When the government unified its three different exchange rates in March 1993, leading to a massive devaluation of the rial from the official level of IR70 to the US dollar to about IR2,700, it steeply inflated the price of imported goods which adversely affected the whole population, irrespective of their income.

Private investment does not flourish without a growing economy, a stable currency and receptive social and political institutions.[13] Iran meets none of these conditions. Foreign investors proved to be in no hurry to invest in such a decrepit economy or in a country with a suspect international political reputation. Iran's myriad Byzantine and contradictory rules and regulations applied to foreign investment has also confused and repelled investors, as has the complex bureaucracy.

Neither the privatisation programme nor the call for the return of émigrés has had much success. The *bonyads* – charitable trusts controlled by clerics and their relatives – have profited the most from the decision to privatise state enterprises by buying them up as soon as they appeared on the market. Private businessmen and industrialists could not compete with these cleric-dominated corporations. Most expatriates who settled comfortably in the West have not flocked back. Many of those who returned have been unable to reclaim their expropriated properties from the religious foundations, or alternatively have found the bureaucratic and judicial red-tape not worth the effort to press their case. Furthermore, émigrés have often felt threatened by the fulminations against them of leading radicals.[14]

The socio-political contradictions have proved equally formidable. Unchecked population growth – from 1979–95, Iran's population has risen from 35m to just over 60m – and massive migration to the cities has put further strain on the deteriorating infrastructure, including housing and educational facilities. Iran has a huge population of young consumers whose material needs are not being satisfied, and who will soon enter the job market, adding to the ranks of the unemployed in a stagnant economy.[15]

President Rafsanjani has proven to be more statist and more cautious than his often outspoken technocratic ministers. As a product of the clerical system he is aware of its slow and cautious *modus operandi*. He cannot move too fast lest the socio-economic effects threaten the power of the clerical regime. Even though statements over the past years have indicated his frustration with the obstacles he faces, he has nonetheless developed a healthy appreciation of them. This was evident in his approach to one of his *bête noires*, subsidies. In April 1994, he contended that some subsidies are extremely costly and do not benefit the poor. Yet he also emphasised that reform in this area must be carried out slowly so as not to sacrifice one of the principles of the Revolution – social justice.[16]

Rafsanjani has cited the experiences of other reforming nations, referring in particular to the problems the Russians are facing as they move from a command to a market economy. Iran could not engage in such a frenetic pace of economic opening and reform. In this context, he pointed to the differences in the speed of reforms undertaken by the former Soviet Union and by China: Gorbachev moved too fast too soon and lost power, while the gradual and cautious 'Chinese position was much more logical than the Soviets'. Rafsanjani added that now 'the Soviets [*sic*] are facing all these problems and the Chinese have maintained their domestic power and strength'. Even so, the Chinese model is not appropriate for Iran because of the many differences between the two countries.[17] In sum, Rafsanjani and his team of technocratic reformers have been working at cross purposes. The technocrats realised that economic reforms required a strong will, determination to stay the course and perseverance regardless of the short-term costs to the population. But they found themselves unable to implement any long-term strategic plan because of political unpredictability and interference by other government departments. This was a criticism voiced by men like Muhammad Hussein Adeli, former Governor of the Central Bank.[18] The technocrats lacked competence and determination, and became increasingly demoralised. Not only have they quarrelled among themselves, highlighting divisions within their ranks, they have also publicly criticised the structural deficiencies of the reform programmes.[19] In addition, they have questioned the President's gradual, politically motivated approach, while some have even threatened to resign their posts.

16

The lack of a social support base for the economic reform pro-grammes significantly restricts the manoeuvrability of Rafsanjani and the technocrats. The mutual incomprehension of the technocrats on the one hand, and the hardliners and conservatives on the other, has been compounded by the alienation of the groups most affected by the restructuring programmes, namely the lower classes, state func-tionaries and the *bazaaris*. The first two groups lament their increasing immiseration, while the *bazaaris* lament the attempt to deprive them of the right to benefit from the existing inequities of the system.

The natural constituency of the technocrats is the remnants of the middle-class *ancien régime*, who have maintained a studied aloof-ness from the Islamic Republic.[20] They have never overcome their dismay at the 'hijacking' of their country by '*akhunds*' (a largely derogatory term for clerics). The middle-class contempt for the clerics' perceived obscurantist social mores, corruption and hypoc-risy continues unabated and is reflected in their acerbic ridicule of the regime. More significantly, the second republic's inability to enforce some measure of political liberalisation or to provide in-centives for expatriates to return from their homes in 'Tehrangeles' (Los Angeles), Paris and Falls Church (Virginia) has been a bitter blow both to the regime's reformers and to the middle class. The latter have withdrawn psychologically further and further into their villas in the suburban enclaves of northern Tehran, behind whose walls they indulge in their taste for things Western, in contraven-tion of the regime's increasingly vocal campaign against the West-ern cultural onslaught. The psychological gap between the Islamic Republic and a large segment of its population could not be wider.

A fundamental problem is the fact that Rafsanjani's political elite has not undergone a 'revolution in consciousness'. Such a group would understand the need for drastic reform and support it un-swervingly, knowing that things would get worse before they got better. The technocratic reformers will fail unless they gain solid support within the power elite. They are backed by the President and by some clerics within the *Majlis*, but in reality the technocrats are an isolated group that cannot manipulate political patronage. The purges of the radicals in the early years of the second republic were not their doing but that of the conservative wing of the clergy. Now it is the technocrats that are being purged.

Obstacles to the Reform Process
As Rafsanjani's economic reforms increasingly impinged on the material interests and institutional positions of those in the power

structure, so resistance to change mounted. A gulf between the interests of President Rafsanjani and the technocrats on the one hand, and those of the Supreme Leader, hardliners and conservative clerics within the *Majlis*, and a vast and inefficient bureaucracy and administrative apparatus, on the other.

President Rafsanjani had underestimated the political aspirations of Ayatollah Khamene'i. Rafsanjani was buoyed, no doubt, by the fact that his partner in the diumvirate, Khamene'i, not only shared his view of the need to reconstruct the country, but similarly lacked the qualifications associated with Ayatollah Khomeini, and would leave the President to run Iran as a powerful executive.[21] But lowering the religious qualifications of the position left Ayatollah Khamene'i no option but to assert his political authority, while striving to improve his religious credentials. Khamene'i fears that growing popular and factional criticism of the austerity and restructuring measures have undermined support for the clerical regime. The President and his supporters also overlooked the potential for Khamene'i to become a magnet for the vested interests threatened by the reforms. Rafsanjani's position was complicated by Khamene'i's tendency – either out of ideological conviction or political calculation – to adopt high-profile public positions close to the radicals and conservatives on both domestic and foreign-policy issues. This not only embarrasses the President, it undermines his strategy.

In the first four years of Rafsanjani's presidency, Khamene'i had not interfered in executive prerogatives, ministerial choices or the direction of the economy in ways that contradicted or hindered his partner. Following the presidential elections of 1993, however, Khamene'i began to exercise his political prerogatives more forcefully. He prevented the President from streamlining the administrative machinery and from purging inefficient public-sector employees, managers and mayors. Khamene'i ensured that his protégés and those of the conservative right remained in charge of high-profile and important ministries or were appointed ministers.[22] The growing prominence of Ayatollah Khamene'i in economic matters was attested to in a letter to the President in late 1993 in which he stated that the government should pay greater attention to the social needs of the people. He recommended improving public services, broadening the social safety net and instituting a progressive tax system that favoured those on low incomes.[23]

The *Majlis* itself has played a key role in challenging economic reforms. Although the radical-dominated third *Majlis* (1988–92) was not as consistently obstructive of Rafsanjani's reform programme as is commonly claimed in Western analyses, the radicals represented an ideological and policy challenge. Invoking the ghost of Ayatollah Khomeini to hinder reform was one of the radicals strongest weapons. With Khomeini's death, the hardline faction, who did not claim to be followers of the Imam's line for symbolic reasons, moved to monopolise the Imam's legacy, calling for undeviating adherence to it. They used this position of ideological purity as a stick with which to beat their opponents on the centre and the right. To compound the problem, the conservatives would often declare that they, and not the hardliners, were the true followers of the Imam. These esoteric political games meant that the technocrats in the middle had to tread carefully so as not to be accused of deviation by either side. Often the technocrats found it necessary to justify or defend their policies. In his speeches, Rafsanjani was compelled to reassure that his policies would not deviate from the line of the Imam, though this situation plainly exasperated him. Despite his enhanced executive powers, much of his energy has been dissipated in fending off such challenges. Intense criticism by hardline newspapers led a frustrated Rafsanjani to comment:

> There are two ways of criticism. One is that you accuse some-
> one of overlooking the values of the Revolution, or of turning
> his back on the policies of the late Imam, or of going against
> Islam. This is a bad method. The [second] reasonable way is to
> prove that a particular action might have certain conse-
> quences. If someone uses this method, it is not displeasing.[24]

Opponents of his policies have taken him at his word and have pointed out the adverse impact of economic adjustment pro-grammes on the population.

The radicals have continued to oppose the economic liberalisation programme because of its harsh impact on the lower classes, and have vigorously opposed the return of the émigrés. They feared having to give expropriated properties back to the returnees, as well as the inflow of Western political and economic ideas and lifestyles. The radicals bitterly opposed Iran's integration into the Western-dominated international economy and delayed the first Five Year Plan in the *Majlis* for six months because of concern over the provision for foreign borrowing.

But the radical faction has severe political weaknesses. It exemplifies the extremism of the 1980s and discredited economic policies. The radicals can no longer mobilise the lower classes as they had done in the war years. They have lost considerable support in the wake of the exposure of their corruption and greed during the Revolution and the war when they exhorted the population to greater sacrifice and martyrdom. The radicals can mobilise people against reform, but cannot mobilise them in favour of anything positive in its stead. Nonetheless, their vocal criticism of his domestic and foreign policies remains a thorn in Rafsanjani's flesh. Mohtashemi claimed in mid-1993 that Rafsanjani's policies had reached a 'dead end'. [25]

In the April 1992, parliamentary elections, Rafsanjani and his *de facto* conservative allies illegally engineered the defeat of the radical faction. This defeat left the conservative right in control of the 270-member legislature. Ironically, the conservative majority in the *Majlis* has been a greater block to reforms than the previous *Majlis*, fearing reforms that threatened the conservatives' material and cultural interests. For the *bazaaris*, an Islamic capitalist system is one of trade and commerce, but not necessarily of rational economic decision-making, nor one in which private industrialists dominate the economy. The *bazaaris* resented the unification of the exchange rates because they had greatly benefited from buying goods at the official rate and re-selling them for vastly inflated prices on the black market. They feared that the government's attempts to rationalise and modernise the tax system would force them to pay higher taxes. Neither the wealthy foundations nor the *bazaaris* wish to see the government bring order and efficiency to Iran's chaotic fiscal system. Lastly, the opponents of the reform measures are increasingly fearful of the impact of the reforms on the lower classes. The riots, demonstrations and strikes that hit cities across the country between 1991 and 1994 have alarmed them. Though many within the political-clerical establishment know that in the long run reforms are essential to preserve the system, in the short term these reforms worsen the plight of almost all economic strata and threaten vested interests and the survival of the system.

The conservatives have obstructed legislation, removed technocratic ministers, and attempted to wrest control of critical areas of the economy from the President. Mindful of the impact of price rises on public transport in the early 1990s, in early 1994 the *Majlis* refused to eliminate the enormous petrol subsidy. The powerful Minister of Finance, Mohsen Nourbaksh, a key player in the economic reform strategy, was ousted by the conservatives after being accused of wanting to preside over the return of Western-style capitalism to Iran.

Rafsanjani's April 1994 tirade against the distorting effects of subsidies on the economy alarmed the *Majlis*. Fearing that the

President was planning further drastic cuts in subsidies and mindful of the impact this would have, the *Majlis* proposed that the government's power to set the prices of goods and services be transferred from the Supreme Economic Council, headed by Rafsanjani, to the *Majlis* itself. Given Rafsanjani's caution – the fact that he has been railing against subsidies for many years seemed to have escaped the *Majlis* – it is unlikely that he would have sanctioned a sudden removal of the subsidy. The following month Rafsanjani backed down from his strictures against subsidies.

Rafsanjani has not developed a firm hold over the levers of government and has proved unable either to control or streamline the worst excesses of the bloated administrative and bureaucratic apparatus. Corruption in the civil service in Iran, as elsewhere, is a result of low public-sector wages, a situation worsened by high inflation. Those who enforce the anti-corruption campaign are corrupt themselves, receiving pay-offs from speculators, businessmen and tax-evaders. The disarray at the top of the political hierarchy over the extent of Iran's serious structural problems is evident even here. While Rafsanjani and the technocrats see corruption as one of the country's most serious problems, Khamene'i seemed unconcerned about it, pointing out that the structure of society is healthy.[26]

To compound the President's problems, a *de facto* alliance has emerged between the radicals and the conservatives who have both attacked the adverse impact of the reform programmes on the population. To both groups, the social distress that the programmes cause erodes the stability of the system. They both abhor, for material and ideological reasons, the call to expatriates to return. Iran's debt crisis has led them to attack the government for Iran's renewed subjugation to Western-based international institutions.

By the mid-1990s, President Rafsanjani's position had been weakened by the structural contradictions inherent in his reform programmes, the adverse social impact of the implemented reforms, and the attack by vested interests on the whole reform strategy. The clearest symbol of Rafsanjani's decline came in the June 1993 presidential elections when he was re-elected for his second and final term. At 57%, the turnout was the lowest ever for the presidency since the establishment of the Islamic Republic in 1979. Rafsanjani faced tougher and more competent opposition – particularly from Ahmed Tavakkoli, a vocal member of the conservative right – than he had in 1989 when his opponent was Abbas Sheybani. In 1989 President Rafsanjani received almost 95% of the vote; in 1993 it fell to 63%. In 1989, just one year after the end of the war with Iraq, Iran was still a mobilised society with a craving for change: Rafsanjani's landslide victory reflected the belief that he could do the job. In 1993, the Islamic Republic had not delivered the goods and that was what mattered to the voting public. Its frustration was reflected in both the low turnout and in the low vote for Rafsanjani. Rumours that the President offered to resign three times in 1994 are hard to confirm, but they only further demoralise those in favour of reforms. Rafsanjani's distress and frustration became clear in May 1994 when he warned that Iran's progress was being obstructed by 'dogmatism'.

The Crisis of Political Legitimacy
Socio-economic problems alone will not lead the Islamic Republic to collapse. Its legitimacy has also been rocked by the contradictions within the political system that emerged following Ayatollah Khomeini's death and by the increasing unpopularity of the clerical rulers. The slow erosion of the Islamic Republic's theocratic foundations over the years has created a crisis of legitimacy for the clerics. Naturally, the secular opposition forces, including intellectuals, in Iran and abroad have always asked, 'why are the clergy entitled to rule?'. But now even the clerics are posing the same question.

The Crisis of the Velayat-e-faqih
The basis of the political legitimacy of the Islamic Republic was the institution of the *velayat-e-faqih* (Guardianship of the Jurisprudent). This innovation in Shi'i jurisprudence was formulated by Ayatollah Khomeini to provide the ideological framework for rule by the jurists. As defined by Ayatollah Khomeini, the *faqih* combines the religious and political qualifications to make him Supreme Leader. As the most senior religious scholar of the Shi'i world – a *marja-e-taqlid* (source of emulation) or senior legal authority by virtue of his knowledge and writings – his edicts are declared as binding on the community of believers. The political qualifications of the jurist include administrative competence and skills to govern the Islamic Republic and to implement divine law, the *Shari'a*. Ayatollah Khomeini had the qualifications to be the *velayat-e-faqih*. Furthermore, his immense charisma and the fact that he was the Revolutionary leader who overthrew the Shah strengthened his political credentials. In retrospect, the position was tailor-made for Ayatollah Khomeini and functioned effectively as long as he occupied it. Many high ranking Shi'i clerics disagreed with the concept of *velayat-e-faqih*, but most chose not to oppose Khomeini directly

and remained steadfastly apolitical. By contrast, none of Khomeini's followers among the political clergy – except possibly Ayatollah Montazeri, who was designated successor to Khomeini until he was abruptly removed – had the religious qualifications to be *marja'*. (The position requires many years of study, published works and acceptance as a source of emulation.)[27]

In this context, it becomes easy to comprehend the tribulations of Supreme Leader, Ayatollah Khamene'i. He has the political qualifications for the position, but lacks the requisite religious qualifications. A mere *hojjatolislam*, or minor cleric, who had devoted his life to political activism and the presidency of the Islamic Republic during the 1980s, Khamene'i was declared Ayatollah and propelled into the post of Supreme Leader after religious qualifications had been declared not essential for it. To make it easy for Ayatollah Khamene'i to accede to the supreme leadership, the collective clerical leadership of the Islamic Republic decided to stress the importance of political qualifications.

Separating the religious authority, *marja'iyat*, from the political leadership, *rahbariyat*, is a major blow to the regime's conception of itself as an Islamic state. The bifurcation of the powers of the Supreme Leader has left Khamene'i in an exposed position in that he lacks Khomeini's jurisprudential authority to settle differences between factions, senior clerics or institutions of state. Not surprisingly then, Khamene'i's political authority was challenged by the radical-dominated *Majlis* in 1989 and 1990. Khamene'i's response to his religiously attenuated position has been to take an activist stance in matters of domestic and foreign policy, usually in favour of the conservatives. But he tried to raise his religious and spiritual stature by issuing edicts of a religious nature: he banned the practice of cutting open the forehead during religious ceremonies, and made a bid to become *marja'*. When Ayatollah Golpeygani died in December 1993, the *marja'iya* passed to 103-year-old Ayatollah Araki, while Khamene'i marshalled support to accede to the position upon Araki's death. Araki died in November 1994 and Khamene'i's machinations were met with outright ridicule and hostility by clerics, both in Iran and the rest of the Shi'i world, who resented this ploy that would have devalued the prestige and position of the senior Shi'i hierarchy. Khamene'i backed down to avoid an acrimonious split in the ranks of the Shi'i clergy and a bruising fight between the state and the clerical establishment. Yet by doing so, Khamene'i did not succeed in resolving the contradictions inherent in his position.[28]

The Corruption of the Political Clergy

Ayatollah Khomeini created a state power structure made up of clerical followers from the lower ranks. Many of these junior mullahs and intermediate *hojjatolislams* had been fanatical and devoted followers of Ayatollah Khomeini even before the Revolution.[29] For these 'political clerics', traditional and apolitical Shi'ism was exemplified by religious scholars wedded to obscure dogmas and political quietism, and whose course of study required years of learning in religious universities. Such a lifestyle held no attraction for the junior clerics who sought their rewards in political power rather than doctrinal studies.

The Islamic state provided them with access to political power and material wealth. Khomeini appointed his supporters to lead congregational Friday prayers in cities throughout Iran where they supplanted local clerics who were perceived as disloyal to the regime. Congregational Friday prayers, which were well attended in the early days of the Revolution, allowed the political clergy to impart the regime's ideology to the people, keep a tight watch over the political pulse of the nation, and use these gatherings as a forum for the mobilisation of the faithful. The clerics infiltrated the state bureaucracy and administration, transforming themselves into a corps of civil servants who ensured state institutions conformed with the ideological vision of the Revolution.

The political clergy abused its power and amassed great wealth, which contributed to the growing chasm between themselves and the traditional clergy. This gap owes less to the traditionalists' resentment of the political clergy's material privileges and access to political power than to their belief that the political clergy are debasing the spiritual value of the clerical establishment by their politicisation and corrupt behaviour. The traditionalists were alarmed by the political clergy's attempt to bring the religious schools under state control, prompting Ayatollah Montazeri into a fierce denunciation of the state's attempts to deprive the clergy of its traditional independence, as has happened in Sunni countries. This unbridgeable gap between the political and traditional clergy has challenged the regime's entire conception of itself as a religious entity.

The masses are increasingly alienated from the clergy. Historically, popular views of the clergy were shaped by contradictory perceptions: rampant anti-clericalism co-existed uneasily with the clergy's position as the institution to whom people turned for spiritual comfort *vis-à-vis* the rulers. Now the clerics themselves are the state. Combined with their impiety, lax morals, corruption and institutionalisation of a 'bureaucratic religion' overly concerned with the outward manifestation of religion – such as conformity with strict social mores – the position and behaviour of the clergy is leading to a mass withdrawal from public religion. Declining attendance in mosques and Friday congregational prayers, and cancellation of pro-government rallies, are the barometer of this alienation.[30] The growing psychological gap between the rulers and the masses on whom they had relied for their legitimacy has been increasingly discussed by Iranian intellectuals, officers of the armed forces, and even influential senior clerics within the political establishment. These critics have all argued that the greed and hypocrisy of the political clergy have besmirched the name of Iran and Islam.

Centre–Periphery Relations
Drug traffickers and unassimilated refugees existing side-by-side with disgruntled ethno-sectarian minorities have contributed to a tremendous lapse of security and stability in Iran's peripheral regions. Iran borders two of the world's biggest drug producers, Afghanistan and Pakistan. The corruption of law-enforcement agencies in Pakistan and eastern Iran, the breakdown of the Afghan state, the emergence of weak states in the former Soviet Central Asian republics, and the proliferation of weapons in the remote border regions have permitted the almost unhindered expansion of drug routes in eastern Iran.[31]

Since 1979, Iran has absorbed over four million displaced persons as a result of war and civil strife in other countries. It has been home to almost three million Afghan refugees since the Soviet invasion of Afghanistan in 1979, and to a large population of Iraqi political refugees who had either been expelled or had fled from Iraq over the previous decade. The massive influx of displaced persons from the Kurdish and Shi'i regions of Iraq after the Gulf War created an additional burden that Iran was ill-equipped to handle. The influx of refugees has resulted in serious security and socio-economic problems. Afghans have earned the contempt and hatred of the local population which blames them for a host of social ills, including violent crime and rape.[32]

Sunni Minorities
Despite the overwhelming domination of the country by Persians and the strong centralising tendencies of Iranian governments this

century, Iran is a mosaic of ethnic, religious and social minorities that make up almost half its population. The modernisation process under the Pahlavis only superficially integrated minority groups and did not relieve the relative backwardness of periphery groups.[33] When the Pahlavi state collapsed, there was a temporary weakening of power at the centre that prompted Iran's periphery – as it had often done in the past – to seek greater autonomy from Tehran. Khomeini's insensitivity to ethnic minorities was guaranteed to cause problems between them and the new Islamic Republic.

Iran's ethnic minorities differ from one another in terms of historical development and in the strength of their respective quests for autonomy. But they do share certain characteristics that have made the minorities a serious security risk: they live in border areas, they are transborder minorities (for example, Iranian Kurds live across the border from Iraqi Kurds), and, in the case of Kurds, Turkomen and Baluchis, they are Sunnis. Economically and politically discriminated against, Sunni areas have had limited interaction with the central government, have the worst infrastructure and the lowest standard of living in Iran.[34] Sunnis are viewed with an atavistic suspicion and hostility by Shi'is for historical and religious reasons. Notwithstanding Ayatollah Khomeini's declaration that 'no difference exists in our Revolution between these two groups', the spectre of sectarianism haunts the Islamic Republic.[35]

Iranian Sunnis, 10% of the population, are the largest religious minority in a Shi'i state. Ayatollah Khomeini and the Islamic Republic have maintained that Islam is one and indivisible with international and national distinctions between Muslims. Non-Muslim minorities are 'protected' second-class citizens, with political representation in the *Majlis*, but Sunni Muslims have no such representation. For the Islamic Republic, Iranian Sunnis – Baluchis, Arabs (in the Bandar Lengeh area), Turkomen and Kurds – constitute a threat because in the early days of the Islamic Republic they engaged in insurgencies in remote border regions. Their existence as Sunnis in a Shi'i state poses a religious, political and security dilemma for a state that has yet to integrate them actively into the body politic. The Islamic Republic cannot ignore the potential for Sunni disturbances to escalate precisely because they inhabit peripheral regions bordering Sunni neighbours.[36]

The Islamic Republic may witness a further rise in the number of peripheral insurgencies that had caused it considerable security problems in the early 1980s. But this time the attacks will be defined in ethnic and, increasingly, in sectarian terms, pitting

Sunnis against the Shi'i state. Kurdish unrest has continued despite the loss of important Kurdish leaders. The province of Khorasan has become Sunni by default, because of its Turkoman minority and the large and destabilising Afghan refugee population. The government is convinced that periodic riots in the province have been instigated or supported not only by the *Mujahedin-e-Khalq* (MKO), which almost invariably appears on the usual list of suspects, but also by Sunnis acting in concert with outside forces.[37] The June 1994 large bomb explosion at the Shi'i shrine of Imam Reza in Mashhad was almost certainly the work of Sunni extremists based in Peshawar, Pakistan, and not that of the MKO as Tehran, which seeks any means to discredit the MKO, hurriedly claimed.[38]

Simmering discontent among the Sunnis of Baluchistan province – a large and backward region lacking adequate infrastructure – has erupted in clashes close to the Pakistan border between regular army troops and the *Pasdaran-i-inqilab-i-islami*, the Islamic Revolutionary Guards Corps (IRGC).[39] Riots erupted in Zahedan in 1994 when Sunni school teachers were replaced by Shi'is. Rumours that a Sunni mosque had been demolished in Mashhad to make way for a Shi'i shrine contributed to disturbances in which rioters set fire to government buildings. Despite official attempts to downplay the significance of the regional Sunni problem, the Islamic Republic's growing concern over any manifestations of the Sunni–Shi'i schism prompted Rafsanjani to stress the need for unity between Sunnis and Shi'is.[40] Tehran's policy towards the regions will continue to be one of carrot and stick. Yet both elements of such a strategy suffer from serious problems. Since 1990 the government has increased the number of dedicated rapid-deployment units in the area, but a reluctance on the part of the military, whether regular army or *Pasdaran*, to put down serious low-intensity regional conflict cannot be ruled out.[41] President Rafsanjani's high-profile visit to Baluchistan in early 1995 was designed to draw attention to the government's promise to devote funds to the development of the province. But there is no indication of where the funds will come from.

Sources of Opposition to the Islamic Republic

The clerical regime is facing widespread discontent. Whether this will translate into a revolution remains to be seen. What helps the regime is that it is not facing organised internal political opposition from mass-based groups. The MKO, a self-styled Islamic–Marxist group whose highly motivated adherents waged a devastating campaign of terror and assassination in 1980–81, is unlikely to seize power. Despite its growing political pretensions, a sophisticated media campaign in the West, and its Iraqi-based National Liberation Army, the MKO has been rooted-out as an effective organised group within Iran by a counter-terror campaign unsurpassed in its ferocity in modern Iranian history.[42] The only serious claimant to power in the short term remains the Iranian armed forces.

The Role and Authority of the Military

The clerical regime has always been suspicious of the loyalty of the regular armed forces. Many units joined the Revolution in 1979, while others refused to fire on the people. Nevertheless, the clerics feared the armed forces' counter-Revolutionary potential. Choosing not to dismantle them, the clerics made sure to control the armed forces politically. This, and the fact that the clerics needed a security force against other internal enemies, led to the formation of the *Pasdaran*.

Since the Revolution, the government has gone to great lengths to ensure control over both the armed forces and the *Pasdars* by setting up political and ideological control mechanisms supervised by clerics at all levels. These include the Ideological-Political Directorate, tasked with the ideological indoctrination of the rank-and-file and officer corps, and the Information Security Organisation, tasked with neutralising any sign of potential opposition from within the military.[43]

But there are rumblings of discontent within the armed forces. The grim socio-economic situation threatens its corporate interests; salaries are pitiful, forcing officers to take on second jobs or postpone starting families. Anti-clerical nationalism may be on the rise. The early 1990s saw the emergence of a shadowy opposition group, the Babak Khorramdin Organisation (BKO), named after an ancient Iranian nationalist. The origins of the BKO are shrouded in mystery, but its members are reputedly veterans of the Iran–Iraq War and the group includes officers from both the army and the Revolutionary Guards. By itself the BKO is not a dire threat to the regime, as it has no clearly coherent ideology or widespread appeal within the ranks of the military. Nonetheless, it cannot be discounted that the armed forces' innate sense of nationalism and concern for their country is being increasingly tested. In the summer of 1994, a former officer, Brigadier-General Azizollah Rahimi, caught the attention of the international media and the Iranian government (which subsequently arrested him) when he denounced the clerical regime for its violation of basic human rights, suppression of political freedoms and mismanagement of the economy. Remarkably, he called on the clerics to return to the mosque and to allow a broad-based national salvation government to take over. Rahimi may have been expressing the hidden sentiments of serving officers.

In this context, the reaction of the regular armed forces and of the Revolutionary Guards during and after the August 1994 riots in Qazvin takes on tremendous importance. The refusal of the Qazvin garrison's *Pasdaran* commander – whose duty was to defend the regime against its internal enemies – to use force to put down serious rioting was endorsed by senior officers. Tehran airlifted into Qazvin a special internal rapid-deployment security force, the Ashura Brigade, to quell the disturbances, which they did rather brutally. Army units moved into the city after the rioting had been put down. Not long afterwards, several senior officers, including members of the *Pasdaran* and the security forces, issued a statement warning that quelling popular unrest was not the task of the armed forces. The riots in Qazvin were not an isolated incident; a pervasive and gener-alised sense of alienation exists in urban centres throughout the country, as illustrated by outbreaks of violence in many cities since 1990.[44]

In the mid-1990s, the ruling elite of the Islamic Republic is no longer concerned with using effective governance to implement its socio-economic and political vision of society, but with the most effective way to ensure the survival of the regime. As if its domestic problems were not enough, the leadership of the Islamic Republic is more susceptible to foreign pressures – which it has so far managed to stave off – than at any time in the past.

II. THE REGIONAL AND INTERNATIONAL CONTEXT

Ayatollah Khomeini set the foreign-policy agenda of the Islamic Republic during the first decade of its existence. Iran's defeat in the war with Iraq heralded the end of the militant attempt to 'export the revolution' by force. Iran's July 1988 acceptance of United Nations Security Council Resolution 598 calling for a cease-fire with Iraq was the revolutionary leader's single greatest submission to the logic of *realpolitik*. But the foreign policy of the second republic has not lived up to expectations that a chastened and devastated Islamic Republic would be transformed into a 'normal' post-revolutionary state.

Foreign Policy of the Second Republic
Foreign-Policy Goals
The second republic's basic policy guidelines stressed that the concrete needs of the post-war Iranian state were to have precedence over abstract revolutionary goals and that Iran would give up extremist rhetoric and ideological slogans. The pragmatists articulated a set of foreign-policy goals: development of 'normal' diplomatic relations with the outside world; improvement of access to Western technology; and integration of Iran into the global capitalist system to enhance economy development. The result would transform the Islamic Republic into a success story that the rest of the Muslim world would try to emulate. According to the pragmatists, domestic economic success would ensure the peaceful export of the Islamic Revolution. But the elite did not universally share these aims, and the pragmatists could not prevent the radicals from calling them a betrayal of the revolution, and even sabotaging them.

Foreign-Policy Apparatus
The second republic's foreign-policy formulation and conduct has been held up for a variety of reasons, mainly domestic in origin. Factionalism, the multiplicity of institutions playing a foreign-policy role and the lack of a single dominant personality make it difficult for the second republic to follow a consistent foreign-policy agenda.

There is a tendency on the part of unofficial institutions including 'charitable' religious organisations like the *Bonyad-e-Musta'azafin* and *Bonyad-e-15 Khordad* to intervene in the foreign-policy arena. The former, which behaves as a law unto itself in Iran, also provides funding to Islamic movements throughout the Middle East. The latter offered to pay the reward for the killing of the British author of *The Satanic Verses*, Salman Rushdie. Such organisations do not come under the control of the President nor of official organs like the Foreign Ministry. Thus, while Rafsanjani cannot revoke the *fatwa* – the religious edict condemning the British author to death for blasphemy – he tried unsuccessfully to dissolve the *Bonyad-e-15 Khordad*. He eventually bypassed the problem by declaring that no official state organ would carry out the sentence against Rushdie. It is thus significant that the sixth anniversary of the issuance of the *fatwa* (February 1995) passed with little commentary on the part of the British or the Iranian governments.

Supreme Leader Ayatollah Khamene'i plays an important role in the foreign-policy process. His lack of religious qualifications and the increased stress on the political and administrative aspects of his position have ensured his strong foreign-policy role. While he shares Rafsanjani's commitment to reconstruction and development, Khamene'i has a genuinely conservative ideological outlook towards the outside world reflected in his exhortations for the Islamic Republic to combat post-Cold War US hegemony, the cultural onslaught against Iran, and Western political and economic domination of the Islamic world.

The President's role in foreign policy has not lived up to the expectations of reformers or of Rafsanjani himself. The enhancement of the President's powers in 1989 was intended not only to strengthen his domestic authority, but also to bring greater direction to foreign policy. The elimination of the post of prime minister was intended to prevent a repetition of the struggle between the two executives in the 1980s. Nonetheless, Rafsanjani has had to tread carefully in foreign-policy matters, especially regarding relations with the United States. Since 1989, radicals have watched closely for any hints of a diplomatic opening towards the 'Great Satan', particularly as Rafsanjani was largely responsible for the infamous 'arms for hostages' controversy in 1987. Rafsanjani has not escaped severe criticism for advocating trade and commercial links with the United States, and Supreme Leader Khamene'i reminded him in no uncertain terms that 'trade was not separate from politics and diplomacy'.[1]

The constitutional reforms of 1989 called for the creation of a Supreme National Security Council (SNSC) headed by the President. It also included two representatives of the Supreme Leader, the head of the judiciary, the Chief of the General Staff, the head of the Plan and Budget Organisation, and the ministers of the Interior, Foreign Affairs, and Intelligence. The SNSC was designed to ensure coordination between national-security matters and foreign policy, and better cooperation between the various foreign-policy institutions. The discretion of SNSC deliberations was reflected in Iran's adoption of prudent policies in two areas of supreme import for the country's national security and foreign policy: the Kuwait crisis of 1990–91; and the collapse of the Soviet Union and subsequent emergence of independent states on Iran's northern border.

The Foreign Ministry's stature had been considerably damaged by the revolution: hundreds of experienced diplomats were purged and replaced in the first republic by semi-literate revolutionary ideologues bent on exporting the revolution and alienating other countries. In the second republic, the Foreign Ministry's position has improved considerably. The end of the war with Iraq in 1988 removed the excessive focus on national security, while the defeat of the export of revolution gave the Foreign Ministry a chance to practise 'normal' diplomacy again. Foreign Minister Ali Akbar Velayati – a medical doctor when he assumed the post in 1981, but now a veteran diplomat – tried to bring a measure of stability to Iran's foreign policy. In recent years he purged many ideologues, improved the research capabilities of the Foreign Ministry (partly by creating the affiliated Institute for Political and International Studies several years ago), and has given the Foreign Ministry a much higher profile through his participation in international events.

The role of the *Majlis* in foreign policy is technically limited to legislative oversight and scrutiny of international agreements to ensure that they do not conflict with Iran's national interests and ideological principles. But the *Majlis* has demonstrated that it is a power to be reckoned with in foreign policy. It can summon for questioning on policy matters cabinet ministers chosen by the President. This capability has constrained the executive's domestic and foreign policies. For example, while the *Majlis* could dismiss Foreign Minister Velayati, it has instead made his tenure more difficult by forcing him to 'explain' certain policies or initiatives, like the invitation to Romania's President Nicolai Ceauşescu to visit Iran on the eve of his downfall in 1989. Also given the poor state of relations between Egypt and the Islamic Republic, Velayati's presence at the Non-Aligned Conference in Cairo in June 1994 was attacked by radicals and certain *Majlis* members.[2]

It is extremely difficult to ascertain the exact foreign-policy roles of Iran's intelligence services – particularly that of the Ministry of Information and Intelligence, but also of the Military Intelligence and the Revolutionary Guards intelligence units. Their activities – including scientific and technological espionage and covert acquisition of dual-use technology, spying on large expatriate Iranian communities in France, Germany and Scandinavia, and assassinating high-profile Iranian dissidents in Western Europe – have contributed to the perpetuation of Iran's negative image in the West. Western intelligence agencies and governments believe these activities are not conducted by 'rogue' elements within Iran, but are formulated at the highest government levels, and their implementation requires the coordination of personnel from several ministries – including Foreign Ministry personnel overseas.[3]

The second republic has no one of Ayatollah Khomeini's stature to dominate decisively the foreign-policy arena. Neither Supreme Leader Khamene'i nor President Rafsanjani have been able to rise above the constraints of a system in which policy is the product of compromise among various institutions and competing factions.[4]

Foreign Policy in Practice
Regional and International Policies 1988–90
Between the end of the Iran–Iraq War and the Kuwait crisis, containment of Iraq was the principal objective of Iranian regional national-security policy.[5] Even as the cease-fire stabilised and the threat of renewed hostilities receded, Iraq continued to rearm and widen the military gap between itself and Iran. Iraq's determination to maintain supremacy over Iran, establish itself as regional gendarme in the Persian Gulf and become the dominant power in the Arab world, was viewed by Iran as a national-security threat and a constraint on its regional diplomacy.

In addition to rebuilding its military, Iran sought to drive a wedge between Iraq and its erstwhile conservative Arab supporters in the Persian Gulf. This could only succeed if Iran did not give these states a reason to see Iraq as a necessary bulwark against a threatening Islamic Republic. Iran also viewed the dependence of these states on foreign powers as another source of instability. Recognising that much of this dependence stemmed from their fear of the Islamic Republic (unwarranted in Tehran's view), the Iranians sought to allay those fears by showing that it was serious about turning over a new leaf in foreign relations. Rafsanjani proposed long-term cooperation with the Arabs, and called for expanded political and economic relations. He added that stability and security in the region were possible only through cooperation, and denied that Iran had any intention of wanting to play 'policeman' in the Persian

Gulf.[6] But tentative attempts by the Gulf Arabs to improve relations with Iran were constrained by their residual fears of the Islamic Republic, the lack of relations between the largest of the Gulf Arab states, Saudi Arabia, and Iran, and the fear of a negative reaction by Iraq.

Even after 1988 when the virulence had eased, relations with the West did not improve, as they were subject to intense inter-factional strife in Iran over the evolution of post-revolutionary foreign policy. Even before the emergence of the second republic, the radicals, fearful of the West taking advantage of Iran's weakness, challenged any attempts to initiate an 'open-door' policy. They had the support and sympathy of Ayatollah Khomeini in this obstructionist strategy. Nothing illustrates this better than the Salman Rushdie affair which has done more harm to Iran–Western relations in recent years than any other issue. In issuing the *fatwa*, Khomeini, still smarting from Iran's defeat in the war, intended to revitalise the radical agenda and slow the pragmatists' attempts to open to the West.[7]

Ayatollah Khomeini's death took some of the wind out of the radicals' sails because they could no longer set the foreign-policy agenda. But their residual strength continued to be evident as they berated the pragmatists whenever the second republic seemed set to move closer to the West. In the early days of the second republic, pragmatists like Rafsanjani believed that Iran could play a helpful role in the release of Western hostages held in Lebanon by the pro-Iranian *Hizbollah* group. It was hoped, no doubt, that this would be taken as a sign of Iran's desire to improve relations. But vehement opposition by radicals like Ali Akbar Mohtashemi – instrumental in building up Shi'i resistance to the 1982 Israeli invasion of Lebanon – to suggestions that Tehran could play a constructive role in the release of the Western hostages forced the government to separate the hostage release from Iran's bilateral relations with Western powers, especially the United States. Ayatollah Khamene'i stated in May 1990 that the release of American hostages was a humanitarian issue, and not a signal to establish relations.

Remarkably, a devastating earthquake in the summer of 1990 became the subject of a fierce controversy between radicals and the government when Tehran decided to accept relief aid from all countries except Israel and South Africa. Internally, the debate centred on whether Iran was going to open up to the world or not. The radicals argued that Western aid should not be seen as altruistic humanitarianism, but as an attempt to re-impose their dominance over a prostrate Iran. The pragmatists' victory was illustrated by American aid transport planes landing at Tehran airport and a Khamene'i speech thanking all who had provided aid.

Relations between the Islamic Republic and the United States were constrained by the domestic politics in both countries and ten years of intense mutual demonisation. From the Iranian perspective, relations with the United States were not so much a foreign-policy issue as a domestic one. A pragmatic leader like Rafsanjani could not make an opening towards the United States without affecting his domestic political position. For radicals, an opening was an ideological betrayal of a principal goal of the revolution: the over-throw of the Great Satan's position in Iran. With Iran's defeat in the war with Iraq and the economy severely weakened, the overthrow of the Great Satan remained the clerics' one victory, and continued opposition to the United States, a critical legitimising device. In August 1989, President-elect Rafsanjani advocated a tentative ap-proach to the United States, prompting a riposte from Ayatollah Khamene'i that there would be no negotiations with the US unless it ended its deceitful ways and its support for Israel. There were also concrete reasons for the Islamic Republic to fear the United States. In Tehran's view, the United States had tried to strangle the Iranian revolution in its infancy, helped Iraq in the war, and entered it on Iraq's side in 1987 when it sent the US Navy into the Persian Gulf, and a US warship 'deliberately' shot down an Iranian passen-ger plane in July 1988.

The American tendency to forgive its enemies does not operate in its relations with the Islamic Republic. The take-over of the US embassy in Tehran in 1979 and the humiliating failure of the hos-tage rescue attempt remain potent memories. The Islamic Repub-lic's disruptive behaviour in the Persian Gulf during the war with Iraq and the embarrassment to the Reagan presidency of the Iran-Contra affair – in which arms were traded for hostages – ensured that Iran remained a 'tar-baby' for both Democrats and Republi-cans.

In contrast, Iranian relations with the former Soviet Union have improved. A number of factors were responsible for the emergence of an Irano-Soviet *détente* in 1989. These included the Iranian desire to end its global isolation, the end of the Iran–Iraq War and the dilution of Soviet support for Baghdad, and Moscow's with-drawal from Afghanistan. The Islamic Republic's desire to take advantage of the Soviet decline, evident even in 1989, also prompted Tehran to make an opening towards what had always been considered the 'lesser Satan'. Iran's looming neighbour had always been a military threat but it had never inflamed domestic passions as had the United States. The latter had dominated Iran politically, culturally and economically under the Pahlavis, and it remained the destination of the vast majority of Iranian expatriates. Except for a few intellectual Marxists and members of the communist Tudeh Party, Iranians had never seen Soviet culture or society as worthy of admiration or emulation.

That the Soviet Union was not an ideological threat was evident when Khomeini sent a letter to President Mikhail Gorbachev arguing that the USSR's problems stemmed from the absence of religion and spirituality in people's lives. Khomeini suggested that the Soviet leader consider Islam as an alternative to the discredited Marxist system, instead of falling prey to Western capitalism. But the turning-point in relations was Rafsanjani's June 1989 visit to the Soviet Union. The *Majlis* Speaker – soon to be President – was more interested in the economic and military aspects of bilateral ties than in religion. Particularly noteworthy was the signing of a ten-year economic agreement and an 'Agreement on Technical Co-operation in the Military Sphere' valued at $6bn.[8] This was an important first step in the reconstruction of Iran's military forces in order to meet the Iraqi menace. But the USSR, particularly in its final years, could never play the leading role in Iran's economic revitalisation, and the West would only change its view of the Islamic Republic if Iran could overcome its negative image and behave as a responsible member of the international community.

Iran and the Impact of the Kuwait Crisis
The Kuwait crisis represented both a threat to Iranian national security and a clear-cut opportunity for the pragmatists to marginalise the radical faction and break out of post-Iran–Iraq War isolation and diplomatic weakness.

The Iraqi invasion and annexation of Kuwait on 2 August 1990 justified Iran's concerns over Iraq's unbridled ambitions. In condemning Iraq's aggression, Rafsanjani made it clear that even if the rest of the world tacitly accepted the Iraqi action, Iran would oppose this change in the political geography of the region. The Tehran leadership later took a pragmatic view of the massive injection of Western forces into the Persian Gulf, hoping that it would subdue the Iraqi military threat once and for all. Yet Iran also saw the Western presence as a threat and hoped for the withdrawal of these forces once the crisis had been resolved.

From the beginning of the crisis, Rafsanjani faced hardline opposition. Many hardliners contended that the United States was Iran's real enemy, and that Iran was morally bound to support Iraq. Others, like leading radical cleric Mussavi Kho'iniha, argued that while Iran had no reason to feel sympathy for Kuwait (one of Iraq's leading supporters in the Iran–Iraq War), it should not support Saddam in his rape and pillage of it, and contended that Iraq was guilty of opening the way for a massive build-up of US forces in the Persian Gulf. The weakness of the radical position stemmed from lack of unity, and from having misread the Iranian people's war-weariness and desire to see Iraq get its just rewards. Furthermore, no one could overlook the hypocrisy of a radical position that called in 1988 for the war to continue until Saddam was overthrown, only to support him after the invasion of Kuwait.

The weakness of the radical position ensured that Ayatollah Khamene'i, President Rafsanjani and the SNSC, which adopted a position of neutrality, would formulate the official Iranian stance towards the crisis. Rafsanjani argued that it was not only ideologically impossible for Iran to support Iraq, to do so would compromise Iranian national security. Saddam Hussein was an opportunist; the Kuwait crisis was a conflict between two evils over control of a strategically important resource. Saddam's move to resolve differences with Iran early in the Kuwait crisis resulted in Iraq's acceptance of Iran's conditions for a formal end to the war, including withdrawal from occupied Iranian territory, joint ownership of the contentious Shatt al 'Arab river, and an exchange of prisoners of war. President Rafsanjani allayed the world's fears that Iran was moving closer to Iraq by making it clear that the Kuwait crisis and Iraq's peace offer were two completely separate issues. Iran could not forego this moment of Iraq's strategic vulnerability to extract the best possible concessions without having to concede anything concrete in return. This was also a victory over the radicals: Rafsanjani had managed to accomplish in a few weeks of negotiation what the radicals had failed to do in eight years of war.

After a decade of being castigated as a threat to regional stability and Western interests, international attention and criticism shifted from Iran to Iraq. Wooing Iran became the objective of many powers: the European Union removed economic sanctions against Iran in October 1990, and relations with the conservative Arab states improved. But the Islamic Republic was not able to capitalise on its stance during the Gulf War to ensure that relations with the outside world would continue to improve.

National Security in the 'Near Abroad'

Iran and Post-Gulf War Iraq

The collapse of Iraq as regional superpower eliminated a direct military threat to Iran. But Iraq's post-war attenuated sovereignty, foreign interference in its affairs and domestic uncertainty following two severe rebellions in the Shi'i south and Kurdish north brought about a situation of general turmoil and instability on Iran's borders. Showing a marked reluctance to revert to the shibboleths of the revolutionary decade, Iran did not actively extend aid to the Shi'i rebels in the south, despite pressure by hardliners to do so. The Iranian leadership recognised its limited ability to influence the political situation inside Iraq. Nor was Iran convinced that the Shi'i opposition could or should seize power in Baghdad. Well aware of the potential benefits of Saddam's fall from power, Tehran believed that after Saddam, stability in Iraq could only be guaranteed if all political, ethnic and sectarian groups, including the Ba'ath party, were represented.

Like other states, the Islamic Republic is worried by Saddam's survival. As long as he remains, his foreign and domestic opponents will continue unabated in their quest to overthrow him, perpetuating turmoil and instability on Iran's borders. Yet his overthrow would raise the spectre either of Iraq's fragmentation or of its falling into the hands of pro-Western and conservative Iraqi opposition groups.

Iraq poses a dilemma for the Iranians: an albeit much weakened Iraq still has considerable powers of regeneration and vast intrinsic strengths.[9] The UN's disarmament of Iraq does not inspire Iran's long-term confidence because it is seen as a temporary solution. Iran's preferred option is to see Saddam weakened and his freedom constrained by the West.

Tehran's various attempts to bring about meaningful change in bilateral relations with Iraq have been hostage to deep-seated problems that separate the two very different regimes. Both states are still profoundly suspicious of one another. This stems from historical animosity, the ideological cleavage between a secular regime in Baghdad and a theocratic state in Iran, and the enduring bitterness occasioned by the war itself. Furthermore, Iraq continues to hold an unspecified number of Iranian prisoners of war as a political bargaining chip in its relations with Iran. Iraq has made the return of the planes that fled to Iran during the Gulf War a pressing concern. Iraq's support for the *Mujahideen-e-Khalq* opposition, which has a large military presence on the border with Iran, is a significant irritant in relations. Iraq's tight control over MKO cross-border raids was loosened in 1991 enabling them to raid industrial facilities in Khuzestan and Ilam provinces, for which Tehran ultimately holds Baghdad responsible.[10] Iran justified as self-defence high-profile aerial attacks on MKO bases in Iraq in the early 1990s and a November 1994 surface-to-surface missile attack, a significant escalation on the part of the Iranians. The Islamic Republic made the tactical decision to work with Saddam Hussein because he is in power and because Tehran does not believe the myriad opposition groups to be serious power contenders. In this context, Iraqi–Iranian relations will be characterised by the *ad hoc* management of tensions.

Bilateral Relations with Turkey, Pakistan and Afghanistan
Iran's relations with Turkey, Pakistan and Afghanistan have been motivated primarily, but not exclusively, by Tehran's desire to bring peace and security to its borders.

Iran and Turkey are important trading partners, but bilateral relations have not been close. There is an intrinsic ideological antipathy between the Muslim world's most secular state, Turkey, and its self-professed leading theocratic state, Iran. Ankara has suspected Iranian involvement in the assassination of Iranian dissidents residing in Turkey, and of support for violent Islamist groups within Turkey. Iran, for its part, has suspected Turkey of territorial ambitions in northern Iraq and of grandiose designs in the newly emancipated southern states of the former Soviet Union. More concretely, Tehran feared Turkey's role as the front line of the Western alliance, as exemplified by its membership in the North Atlantic Treaty Organisation, and its use as a base for coalition attacks against Iraq. Nonetheless, by the mid-1990s, bilateral relations had improved substantially, both sides having pulled back from hostile positions. Iran does not want, nor can it afford, to have problems with another neighbour.[11] So determined is Iran to avoid being seen as interfering in Turkey's domestic affairs that Rafsanjani refused to comment on the large municipal-election victories of the Islamist Welfare Party. Both states were concerned about deteriorating border security, as Kurdish guerrillas in Turkey tried to use Iran as a base from which to launch attacks. Both expressed tremendous anxiety over the emergence of the 'Kurdish enclave' in Iraq. In several meetings between high-ranking officials of the two countries, both sides agreed that northern Iraq should not become the base for an independent Kurdish entity that could act as a magnet for restive Kurdish minorities in both Turkey and Iran. Tripartite meetings between Iran, Syria and Turkey reaffirmed a commitment to Iraq's territorial integrity. It remains to be seen whether the major Turkish incursion into northern Iraq in early spring 1995 will have a negative impact on Irano-Turkish relations in light of Tehran's criticism of it. Iran's response may be to increase its own surreptitious activities in northern Iraq to thwart excessive Turkish influence in the region; to prevent any semblance of unity between the two major Iraqi Kurdish groups which are bitter rivals; and to deprive the Iranian Kurdish organisation, the KDPI, of sanctuary in northern Iraq. Iran's aim is ultimately to prevent the export of instability from northern Iraq into traditionally disgruntled Iranian Kurdistan.

Iran's relations with Pakistan are of a different nature than those with Turkey. The issue of border security in Baluchistan, one of Iran's more remote provinces, clearly concerns Tehran's elite. In the 1970s, imperial Iran and Pakistan cooperated in combating Baluchi separatists. They are doing so again in the 1990s, but this time they are also trying to coordinate their struggle against the drug trade. When the Pakistani President undertook a state visit to Iran in 1994, both countries reiterated their determination to work towards increasing security cooperation along their common borders.[12] Iran is also fearful of growing instability in Pakistan and the increase in Sunni–Shi'i sectarian violence in cities like Karachi.

Irano-Pakistani relations are also strategic and military in nature. In 1994, the Iranian and Pakistani navies conducted joint exercises for the first time. Links in the military field would benefit Iran more than Pakistan because the latter has a more formidable military, a more developed arms industry, and a nuclear infrastructure. But Iran is constrained from developing closer relations with Pakistan by its desire not to alienate India, which it views as a major global power and a potentially important economic partner.

Iran's eastern neighbour, Afghanistan, has not known a year of peace since 1979. With the victory of the *Mujahedin* anti-government forces over the Marxist government in early 1992, Iran indicated its preference for a fair distribution of power among all of Afghanistan's ethnic and sectarian groups. Following their victory, the cement binding the various *Mujahedin* groups fell apart and Afghanistan broke into heavily armed warring confessional cantons. This development frustrated important Iranian goals. Resolution of the bloody strife in post-communist Afghanistan would go a long way towards ensuring stability and peace in the Iranian province of

Khorasan because Iran's huge Afghan refugee population – most of which is in Khorasan – could then presumably go home. The perpetuation of conflict in Afghanistan also provides an opportunity for foreign – primarily Saudi and Pakistani – involvement and influence. Furthermore, it is alarming to Tehran that much of this aid goes to 'unsavoury' militant Sunni groups. Iran has been seeking to mediate between the warring parties and expressed its readiness to assist in the country's reconstruction.

Iran and the Post-Soviet Successor States

It was with ill-disguised unease that Iran watched the political situation in the USSR between 1989 and 1991. The collapse of the Soviet Union saw the demise of a hated ideology, the end of a perennial military threat from the north, and opportunities for relations with the newly independent states of the former USSR. But the sudden dissolution of the USSR and its replacement by 15 separate republics, including three weak ones – Armenia, Azerbaijan and Turkmenistan – on Iran's borders, presented Tehran with a new and unstable geopolitical environment that inspired a cautious approach.

Iran feared that the United States would move to fill the power vacuum in Central Asia. It was also alarmed by belief in the West and Middle East that Iran would spearhead a wave of Islamic fundamentalism that would engulf Central Asia, and by the United States' haste to promote Turkey as the political and economic model for the Central Asian states.[13]

Russia continues to be the dominant power in Iran's periphery with strong national-security, political, economic and social interests. Iran recognised this more quickly than Turkey, whose much loftier expectations did not materialise: the once widely espoused view that with the collapse of the USSR, Central Asia would be the arena for a regional 'Great Game' between Turkey and Iran has been proved wrong. Maintaining and strengthening bilateral ties with Russia became a cardinal principle of Iranian diplomacy.[14] The Islamic Republic conducted its policy towards Central Asia cautiously so as not to give Russia cause to believe it was promoting Islamic fundamentalism, using only general reference to cultural links and shared values in its diplomatic relations with them. Iran did not wish to jeopardise its technical and economic links with Russia, as the latter had made clear that these links depended on 'responsible' Iranian behaviour in Central Asia. It also sought to downplay potential differences, as in the case of the war in Bosnia-Herzegovina where Iran is sympathetic to the Bosnian Muslims and

Russia to the Serbs. Instead, Iran has chosen to lambast the West and the UN for not doing enough to save the Muslims. Iran's prudent approach to the civil war between former communists and a coalition of Islamists and nationalists in Tajikistan also illustrates its desire not to antagonise Russia. Iran initially supported the Islamists and nationalists after they had temporarily seized power. But active Russian support for the communists quickly prompted Iran to adopt a low profile. Although Islamist opposition leaders have found refuge in Iran, Tehran pushed hard for a compromise settlement between the two sides.[15] Russia's violent suppression of the Chechen attempt to establish an independent republic in the Caucasus in 1994–95 led Tehran to issue statements simply regretting the bloodshed in Chechnya and the fact that Russia has not been able to solve the crisis peacefully.

To underscore its interest in establishing normal state-to-state relations, Iran has vigorously promoted economic and commercial cooperation with its landlocked neighbours to the north. Almost all major visits by senior Iranian officials to the Central Asian states, including one by Rafsanjani in late 1993, have focused on economic cooperation, commerce, trade and cultural interaction. Iran has offered itself as the primary overland trade route to Gulf ports, providing these states with an alternative to Russia and the conflict-prone Transcaucasus. In this context, Iran attempted to revitalise the Economic Cooperation Council (ECO), whose original membership included Iran, Turkey and Pakistan, and encouraged the Central Asian states to join. Iran hosted the first ECO summit in Tehran in February 1992 with delegates from five former-Soviet states in attendance. Tehran had hoped that an expanded ECO would enhance economic, cultural, political and commercial relations between the original three members and the new states, leading to the creation of an Islamic common market. In light of Iran's severe economic distress, the infrastructural backwardness of the Central Asian states and Russia's continued domination of the area, by the mid-1990s it had become clear that there was no possibility of forming such an economic bloc either in the short or in the medium term.

Instability in and conflict between former Soviet republics in the Caucasus has greatly alarmed Iran, particularly the bloody conflict between Armenia and Azerbaijan over the territory of Nagorno-Karabakh. Initially, Iran supported Christian Armenia to counterbalance Turkish support for their kinsmen and fellow Muslims, the Azeris. By late 1994, a string of Armenian victories that Iran viewed as regionally destabilising, particularly in light of the extensive seizure of Azeri territory, led an alarmed Iran actively to pressure Armenia. In several diplomatic demarches, the Iranian government warned Armenia to pull its forces out of occupied Azeri territory.

Iran's anxiety over the Azeri–Armenian conflict did not arise solely because two of its neighbours were engaged in a war; roughly 20% of Iran's population are Azeris – the largest ethnic group after the Persians – who live close to the conflict zone. Iran's Azeris are Shi'i and have been fully integrated into Iranian society, politics and economic life. But the Islamic Republic feared that Azeri nationalists, whether in the Republic of Azerbaijan or in Iranian Azerbaijan, impelled by disastrous defeats at the hands of the Armenians, might demand the unification of former Soviet Azerbaijan and Iranian Azerbaijan. Tehran sent Azerbaijani refugees back to Azerbaijan as quickly as possible, and has even provided financial aid for the upkeep and maintenance of refugee camps in former Soviet Azerbaijan.[16] The emergence in 1992 of a militantly secular ultra-nationalist Azeri movement in northern Azerbaijan – personified by the Republic of Azerbaijan's second President, Abolfaz Elchibey, who called Iran 'an empire ripe for dissolution' and who looked to Turkey as his model – caused alarm in Tehran.[17] It was with considerable relief that Iran greeted his downfall in 1993 following Azeri defeats to the Armenians.

Iran and Persian Gulf Security
In no other region has the Islamic Republic snatched defeat from the jaws of victory as in the Persian Gulf. Iran's current policy in the Gulf is dictated by nationalism, and economic and politico-strategic interests. These are the three constants in Tehran's Persian Gulf policy, and in this respect, the policy of the Islamic Republic is similar to that of Mohammed Reza Shah.

There is a deeply ingrained historical and mythological Iranian view that the body of water on which Iran has a 2,000 mile coastline is the *Persian* and not the Arabian Gulf. Iran is the most strategically important state in the Persian Gulf by virtue of its historical connection to the waterway; unilateral control of one shore of the Gulf; shared control of the choke-point, the Straits of Hormuz, with the Sultanate of Oman; and demographic and economic weight. The Persian Gulf is also Iran's economic artery to the outside world.[18]

To Tehran, the fact that the Persian Gulf is also the site of vast oil reserves has made it the focus of international attention, rivalry and intrigue in the twentieth century. The result has been insecurity, conflicts and war between littoral states, and interference in Persian Gulf affairs by outside powers. Iran holds that extra-regional powers, including those in the wider Middle East, must be excluded from the Persian Gulf, and that security must remain in the hands of the littoral powers.

Security arrangements based on peaceful interaction and cooperation between neighbouring states will also ensure that the price of oil will not fluctuate, causing bankruptcy and hardship to countries like Iraq and Iran that do not have substantial currency reserves. As Foreign Minister Velayati put it, 'if aliens control our oil prices, events similar to the Kuwaiti crisis will unfold and endanger international peace and security'.[19] The Iranians add that if the littoral states attain regional security and stability by themselves, this would also go a long way towards ensuring that the economic interests of the industrialised world are safeguarded.

Iran expected to be included in any post-Gulf War security arrangement. Plans for an exclusively Arab regional security system in the Persian Gulf, including Arab non-littoral states, raised hackles in Iran. On 6 March 1991, the Gulf Cooperation Council and its two leading Arab allies, Egypt and Syria, issued the Damascus Declaration (Six-plus-Two) stating that Egyptian and Syrian forces already deployed in the Arabian peninsula would constitute the nucleus of an Arab peace force to guarantee the safety and security of the Arab states in the Gulf region. Even when inter-Arab cooperation foundered following Egypt's sudden withdrawal of its forces in May 1991, deep-seated Arab suspicions of Iran, in addition to other developments, dashed hopes for closer Irano-Arab security cooperation. The fears of the Arab states concerning Iranian ambitions, its capacity for 'mischief-making', and its size and power, had never diminished. Their experience with the other large power of the region, Iraq, had increased their wariness of both their big neighbours.

Iran's relations with the Gulf Arabs are also affected by long-standing tensions in relations with Saudi Arabia, the other state in the region that defines itself as an Islamic state. Iran is not attempting to export revolution to its Wahabi neighbour across the sea, but to be morally ascendant in the Islamic world. Iranian relations with Saudi Arabia deteriorated over Saudi attempts to restrict the number of Iranian pilgrims because of their tendency to politicise the *hajj* – pilgrimage to Mecca – with demonstrations against the 'enemies' of Islam.

In spite of the fact that Tehran correctly claims that the Arabs buy more and better weapons systems from the West, Iran's rearmament programme has frightened the Arabs. The Islamic Republic's capabilities and intentions both account for Arab unease. The Gulf Arabs point to a pattern of perceived hostile and muscular Iranian nationalism that has changed little since the period of the Shah, best illustrated by the dispute over the sovereignty of the island of Abu Musa.

In August 1992, Iranian officials suddenly decided to expel foreigners from the island of Abu Musa and refused others permission to land. Under a 1971 agreement signed by Sharjah – a sheikdom of the United Arab Emirates – and Iran, the island was to come under joint sovereignty with Iranian military forces occupying part of the island. Iran's action caused a storm of protest throughout the Arab world and caught the attention of the West (in contrast to the tepid reaction to the Shah's seizure of it in 1971). But Tehran is determined to keep the island irrespective of the damage to its relations with the United Arab Emirates. Furthermore, its fortification of the islands (after the United States moved forces back into Kuwait in October 1994 following yet another crisis with Saddam) has heightened tensions with Arabs who are convinced that Iran has not been transformed into a benign neighbour. The West sees Iran's military presence on the island as a threat to shipping and the security of its own naval forces in the Persian Gulf. Tehran sees the combined Arab–Western opposition on this issue as an attempt to shift attention away from the Arab–Israeli arena where progress is scant. The Abu Musa crisis will not be easily resolved. For the Iranian government and people it is a matter of Iran's national pride and territorial integrity.

International Politics: The Imperatives of Ideology
The second republic cannot entirely escape the constraints imposed by its revolutionary origins and the Islamic ideology it espouses, as its origins are critical to its legitimacy. The Islamic Republic follows a 'dual policy' wherein the logic of state interests and of the revolution coexist uneasily. The inherent tensions between Iran's statist interests and its universalist impulses – which, in a revolutionary state, are an externalisation of domestic politics – are best illustrated in the conduct of its international foreign policy. The impact of domestic political factionalism on foreign policy is evident in the existence of two mutually reinforcing ideological trends that influence Iranian conduct towards the world.

First, there is a counter-offensive against the so-called cultural onslaught by the West. Iranian fear of Western cultural domination is expressed in the writings of Iranian intellectuals and the speeches of the Islamic Republic leadership throughout the 1980s. But the campaign to counter Western 'cultural aggression' was initiated in full force by the conservatives after their *Majlis* victory in April 1992, and it is supported by the Supreme Leader. According to the campaign, the West is trying to undermine the legitimacy and independence of the Islamic Republic by striking at its Islamic cultural foundations through the media and exposure of Iranians to Western lifestyles. Thus enforcing the *chador* (modest Islamic dress for women) and Islamic mores in general – banning satellite dishes that beam in 'filthy' Western programmes; the removal of the head of Iranian Radio and TV for laxity in combating cultural aggression; and a bizarre but short-lived campaign against Coca-Cola in Iran – are linked internal and external elements of this counter-offensive. Although not universally shared, the cultural counter-offensive represents a nexus between those groups ideologically hostile to an opening to the West (the radicals) and those who want economic ties but fear what such an opening could mean to Iran's Islamic cultural and social identity (the conservatives). Furthermore, for these groups, the strategy is another way to wage 'war' against the United States which, as the state whose cultural domain is truly global, is the spearhead of the cultural assault.

Second, even though the strategy of exporting the revolution died in 1988, the Iranian leadership still manifests a 'residual revolutionary optimism', and sees the Islamic Revolution as destined to triumph. It seeks to take advantage of a resurgence of Islam throughout the region and perceive the Islamic Republic as the Islamic world's primary opponent of the United States.[20]

The Islamic Republic's behaviour in the Middle East is a serious obstacle to better relations with the West and, above all, the United States. This behaviour includes: Iran's rejection of the legitimacy of the state of Israel; its financial and military support for the Islamic regime in Sudan, suspected by both Arab and Western states of aiding Islamists in Egypt and Algeria; its support for Islamist movements, like *Hizbollah* in Lebanon and *Islamic Jihad* and *Hamas* in the Israeli-occupied territories; and most significantly, its vehement verbal and ideological opposition to the Arab–Israeli peace process, which it sees as a flawed venture into which the Arabs were forced. Several days prior to the convening of the US-sponsored October 1991 Madrid peace conference that brought Arabs and Israelis together, the Islamic Republic held its own rejectionist conference on the Palestine question.

Iranian national-security concerns also played a role in the country's hostile reaction to the peace process, as Tehran feared a diminution in its strategic relationship with Syria if the latter were to normalise relations with Israel. Furthermore, President Assad of Syria would undoubtedly curtail or halt the activities of *Hizbollah* in Syrian-dominated Lebanon. Tehran has curtailed its financial support for *Hizbollah*, urged its leadership not to engage in risky adventures against Israel, and encouraged the organisation to play a constructive role in Lebanese politics. Nonetheless, *Hizbollah*'s paramilitary operations in southern Lebanon against Israel and its Lebanese allies enables Tehran to claim that Islamic forces are successfully engaging the 'Zionist entity'.

Iran also opposes the Arab–Israeli peace process for a seemingly irrational reason, but one that is intricately tied up with its confrontation with the Great Satan: the United States has staked its reputation on the success of the peace process. For that reason, the Islamic Republic wants to see it fail. This approach has earned Iran the wrath of the United States. Confronting the Great Satan is simply one of the few remaining legitimising symbols for the Islamic Republic; it has also become an emotional crutch in the aftermath of the Cold War and the rise of the United States to the status of sole superpower. The enhancement of US political and military power in the Persian Gulf following the Gulf War has caused tremendous anxiety in Iran.[21] The strengthening of US political and strategic relationships with Gulf Arab states and enhancement of its ability to strike at Iran militarily or to wage economic warfare against it constrain Iran's freedom of manoeuvre in the Persian Gulf region.

Relations between Iran and the United States further deteriorated between late 1992 and early 1995. In its final months, the Bush administration relinquished its initial strategy of reaching out to Iranian 'moderates' in the hope that 'goodwill begets goodwill'. It finally chose to steer clear of the Islamic Republic, and castigated it for its support of terrorism, opposition to the Arab–Israeli peace process and rearmament programmes.

This shift presaged the approach of the Clinton administration (which took office in January 1993). In May, the new administration unveiled an ambitious plan called the 'dual containment' policy (DCP) to deal with perceived threats posed by Iran and Iraq to regional security and US interests in the Middle East. Adopting as a starting point the need to protect US strategic interests and allies in the Persian Gulf, the DCP explicitly rejected the old strategy of balancing the power of Iran and Iraq, as had been done during the

Iran–Iraq War. This could no longer work, as both Iran and Iraq were implacably hostile to the United States.

Instead, the US, in concert with its allies and friends, would put military and economic pressure on both countries to bring about a change of government in Iraq and a modification in the behaviour of the Islamic Republic. The DCP called upon Iran to halt its support for and sponsorship of terrorism throughout the world; attempts to thwart the Arab–Israeli peace process; subversion of Arab regimes friendly to the United States; acquisition of offensive conventional weapons; and its quest to acquire weapons of mass destruction. Once Iran's policies change, the United States would be willing to normalise relations with an Islamic Republic whose legitimacy the United States fully recognised.[22]

Iran claimed that DCP signified a US retreat, because until then the US policy intent was to overthrow the Islamic Republic. Iran stridently refuted the charges against it. Furthermore, its leadership declared that for Iran to submit to US dictates would be to deprive the Islamic revolution of its credibility and political independence. But more important than any Iranian reaction to the DCP was the fact that it suffered from internal contradictions.

DCP assumed a consensus within the Islamic Republic on an across-the-board normalisation of relations with the United States. This consensus does not exist, as some groups were adamantly against normalisation, while others thought they could have trade and commercial relations without inviting the Great Satan diplomatically back into Iran. In fact, some Iranians declared that a restoration of relations with the United States would not solve Iran's economic problems. More significantly, DCP found no supporters among the United States' major allies and other powers like Russia and China. Iran's strategy was to ensure that other major powers would not follow the US line, and it actively sought to improve its political and economic relations with the major Western partners of the United States – Russia and China. These powers did not see Iran as the embodiment of evil and always demanded evidence to back up claims of egregious Iranian behaviour. The moral force of the DCP was undercut by the fact that the United States was one of Iran's biggest trading partners, which the Europeans lost no time in pointing out to the United States. Although wary of unsavoury Iranian behaviour and dismayed by its negative attitude to the Arab–Israeli peace process, the Western Europeans and Japanese chose to adopt an *ad hoc* policy of 'constructive engagement'. This entailed creating a web of diplomatic and economic ties with the Islamic Republic in the hope of modifying its behaviour. There were strong arguments for Europeans to favour maintaining and enhancing links with the Islamic Republic. Iran was a lucrative market of 60 million people, and it owed the Europeans several billion dollars in short-term debt – which the Europeans re-scheduled into less onerous medium-term debt (despite US pressure not to do so).

By early 1995, developments in the United States and Middle East rendered meaningful dialogue between the US and Iran less likely. The Clinton administration came under pressure from a more hawkish Congress to toughen its stance towards the Islamic Republic. Regional developments in the Middle East, including Iran's perceived muscle-flexing in the Persian Gulf, worried the United States more than it did the local powers, but highlighted the Iranian rearmament programme. The dormant status of the Arab–Israeli peace process due to a surge of terrorism linked to Iran on the basis of its opposition to the process, and the view in Tel Aviv of Iran as the greatest threat to Israel's national security, have contributed to the growing hostility towards Iran. Though the demonisation of the Islamic Republic has reached new heights, Tehran is not blameless. Its inability to jettison the more unsavoury aspects of its diplomacy, its gratuitous opposition to the Arab–Israeli peace process and the legitimacy of Israel and, lastly, its inability to devise a coherent counter-strategy have hurt it considerably.

III. IRANIAN DEFENCE POLICIES

The quest for an effective national military establishment has pre-occupied Iranian rulers for the past 200 years.[1] Like their predecessors the Pahlavis, the Islamic Republic's rulers recognised the need to establish effective armed forces. But the Iran–Iraq War intruded before they could rebuild the military capabilities destroyed during the Revolution. Despite superior morale and initiative, the Iranian war machine suffered from a multiplicity of military forces that often acted at cross-purposes. It was also constrained by the arms embargo on Iran, and the leadership's low-technology military strategy, adopted partly out of the ideological belief held by the radicals – who dominated the formulation of Iran's strategy – that morale, faith and fervour were more important than weapons and technology. Towards the end of his life, Ayatollah Khomeini repeatedly emphasised the need to rebuild Iran's military power. Following his death, it was left to the second republic's technocrats and pragmatists to assess military needs and devise a rearmament strategy.

Rearmament Strategies of the Second Republic
Rebuilding Iran's shattered post-war military was one of the second republic's primary tasks. It was to be undertaken in conjunction with economic development, and an opening to the outside world. All three were part of a comprehensive reconstruction strategy.[2]

The rearmament strategy was three-pronged. First, it called for the reorganisation and selective rebuilding of the conventional armed forces. The end of the war with Iraq did not make it easier to acquire new weapons systems. Western states still maintained an unofficial embargo which, with their growing suspicion of Iran's intentions, had taken on an air of permanence by the mid-1990s. Prior to the collapse of the Eastern bloc, Iran tried to acquire weapons from states like Poland, Czechoslovakia, Yugoslavia and Romania. Iran hoped that Czechoslovakia would provide 200 T-54/55 tanks and construct a factory to produce anti-tank weapons, while Poland and Romania would provide several hundred tanks to replenish Iran's seriously depleted armoured inventory.[3] But attempts to establish an arms trade with the Eastern bloc came apart following the revolutions of 1989–90 and the unravelling of Yugoslavia. Furthermore, Iran cannot finance, nor does it have the international support to implement, a strategy of massive arms acquisitions from abroad, and this will dictate the nature and pace of the technocrats' rearmament plans for the remainder of the 1990s.

Second, the development of Iran's defence industries to ease dependency on foreign suppliers has been a cardinal principle of the Islamic Republic. The defence industries' achievements have been remarkable, but Iran has tended to exaggerate them, while underestimating structural deficiencies and constraints.

Third, Iran's experiences in the Iran–Iraq War and the lessons of the Gulf War have led it to attempt either to produce or acquire weapons of mass destruction to obtain a deterrent and retaliatory capability. But the development of WMD is also beset by structural deficiencies, like an unsophisticated defence industrial base and low research and development (R&D) capabilities, while the attempted acquisition of WMD, particularly ballistic missiles, has been held back by intense foreign pressure and financial stringency.

Reconstructing Conventional Power
Rebuilding Iranian Air Power
The Iranians perceive the Air Force to be at the forefront of rapid deployment against the forces of a potential enemy.[4] The Iranian Air Force was the most prepared of the regular military branches when the war with Iraq broke out.[5] This fact alone has ensured that it remains pivotal in Iranian military thinking. It has led to attempts to halt and reverse the chronic decline in operational capabilities that occurred during the war with Iraq. In 1986, Iran instituted a 15-year plan for long-term recovery and rebuilding of Air Force capabilities under Air Force Commander Mansur Sattari. (Sattari died along with several other high-ranking officers in a January 1995 aircraft accident.)[6] At the end of the Iran–Iraq War, President Rafsanjani reiterated the importance of the Air Force, stating that in spite of the end of the war, it 'should still remain strong so that no one will entertain any thoughts of attacking this country'. He added:

> the government and the *Majlis* have seen the strength of the Air Force in the war ... they will strive to complete its offensive and defensive chain ... and the Air Force will be one of the strongest forces in the region in the future.[7]

The Air Force modernisation plan called for establishing an indigenous scientific and technical infrastructure, continued upkeep of the remaining US planes and acquisition of new planes. An aeronautical university was established to meet the pressing need for pilots, warrant officers, technicians, ground crew and engineers. By building a domestic aeronautics infrastructure, the Iranians have been able to avoid squandering scarce resources to train them abroad, 'contamination' of the Air Force by foreign ideas, and importing foreign specialists.[8]

Keeping the inventory of American-built fighters (which Iran values highly) air-worthy for as long as possible is the foremost priority. Due to a lack of spare parts, degraded avionics and inoperable weapons systems many of these planes are not combat-capable and have been mothballed. The former Defence and Logistics Minister, Akbar Torkan, has said that Iran can keep them flying for another 20 years if it ensures a high level of maintenance, and if it can obtain upgraded avionics and spare parts.[9] Iran has had some success in upgrading and providing spare parts for the fleet of F-4s and F-5s without recourse to the United States, as there is a sizeable global inventory of these planes.

The Iranians will face a dilemma when their fleet of US-made planes dwindles and becomes obsolete in the next five years. Given the tenor of Iranian–US relations, the United States will not provide Iran with high-performance fighters in the foreseeable future. The only other large-scale suppliers are China and Russia. The Chinese, for whom the Iranians are full of contempt, specialise in the production of obsolete and high-maintenance fighter planes. Financially strapped Russia has proved willing to sell high-quality fighters. The first significant arms deal with the Soviet Union came in mid-1989 when it agreed to sell Iran a squadron of MiG-29 *Fulcrum* air-superiority fighters, and to assist in establishing an air-defence network.

Much has been written about the unexpected 'gift' of 91 Soviet-built Iraqi warplanes that fled to Iran at the height of the coalition aerial assault on Iraq in January 1991.[10] Contrary to early reports, not all of them have enhanced the power of the Iranian Air Force. Half of the planes are obsolete SU-20/22s. The planes were flown to Iran without logistical support, spare parts or maintenance manuals. At the time, Iran had a squadron of modern Soviet planes that it was just beginning to integrate into its force structure; but it did not have a sufficient number of Soviet-trained pilots or ground crews to maintain the approximately four squadrons that appeared out of the blue. Nonetheless, the more modern planes, like the MiG-29s and SU-24s, have been successfully integrated into the Iranian Air Force.

Commander Sattari's July 1991 visit to Moscow culminated in a $6bn arms deal designed to re-equip the Iranian Air Force and ground forces. The agreement allegedly called for the delivery of an additional 100 MiG-29s, construction of a MiG assembly plant, and delivery of a squadron of SU-24s to supplement the squadron of Iraqi ones. Military links between Iran and the USSR were not severed following the Soviet Union's collapse. But due to financial constraints, Iran has not been able to acquire all it had on its 1991 'wish list'.

There are threats, however, to the stability of the Russo-Iranian arms relationship. While it is designing high-quality fighters, and its latest generation of war planes have received high praise at international air shows, Russia poses tremendous problems as an arms supplier. It cannot be relied upon for prompt delivery of weapons, spare parts and technical advice. Russia is also susceptible to pressure from the West and could be persuaded to reconsider its arms relationship with the Islamic Republic. The Clinton administration has tried to pressure Russian President Boris Yeltsin into terminating its arms trade with Iran. Although Russia has promised to do so, it insists that existing contracts (which could be backed-up for years) must be honoured. Russo-Iranian relations could deteriorate because of political differences in Central Asia and instability in the Caucasus. Russian Foreign Ministry officials have made it clear that the continuation of good Russo-Iranian relations depends on 'responsible' Iranian behaviour in Central Asia.[11]

Iran's air defences have traditionally been the weakest of the armed forces. Deficiencies that existed in the 1970s – poor radar coverage, lack of automatic data processing, and a weak integrated anti-aircraft missile system – have not been rectified in the Islamic Republic. The poor state of Iran's air defences enabled Iraq to use slow and otherwise obsolete bombers to fire from high altitude with impunity during the war. An air force more competent than Iraq's would have been able to inflict far more damage on Iran. In February 1992, the Iranians finally received their first SA-5 *Gammon* long-range surface-to-air missiles (SAMs).

Revitalising Iranian Naval Power
During the Iran–Iraq War, the Iranian Navy protected Iran's merchant marine, defeated Iraq's Navy and shut down Iraqi ports.[12] The Persian Gulf continues to be critical to Iran's national security.[13] This was well articulated by Foreign Minister Velayati in his statement that 'our most important strategic border is our southern coastline, the Gulf, the Straits of Hormuz and the Sea of Oman. We cannot remain indifferent to its fate'.[14] Iran has always considered the Persian Gulf *mare nostrum*. More concretely, it is Iran's only export route for oil, on which it depends for its economic well-

being. Iran painfully remembers Iraq's attempts to throttle its oil exports from the Gulf during the Iran–Iraq War. Iran's petrochemical infrastructure, oilfields and oil-export terminals are all located on or near the Gulf. And, it is the only area where Iranian and American forces operate in close proximity, causing distinct unease to Iran. The presence of US naval units in the Gulf is a symbol of Iranian military impotence, and a constant reminder of its effectiveness against Iran in 1988. US naval power would undoubtedly be the spearhead of any punitive American action against Iran.[15] Thus the rebuilding of the Navy is intended to protect economic interests and to enhance national security on the southern flank.[16]

Although Iran's Navy is the largest in the Persian Gulf, it suffers from severe weaknesses. Its major surface vessels are either obsolete or are not fully seaworthy because they lack functioning radar or electronic subsystems. The Navy faces a severe shortage of modern anti-ship and anti-aircraft missiles, and it has no significant naval air arm.[17] Iran does not have the financial resources to engage in a major refurbishment of its surface combatants, and there have been no reported orders for large surface combatants.

The various naval exercises that have taken place since 1988 may indicate Iran's determination to show that it is capable of projecting naval power in the Persian Gulf; to thwart enemy operations close to its shore; and to rectify serious deficiencies uncovered during the Iran–Iraq War, particularly those that became evident after the a severe assault on Iran by the US Navy in 1987–88. These exercises have grown larger each year. By the mid-1990s, Iran was able to demonstrate operation and coordination of ground forces, air units, submarines, surface combatants and naval commandos.

Iran's acquisition of naval weaponry has been selective and modest, but nevertheless quite threatening to outside powers. Iran is acquiring cruise missiles for naval use in addition to the Chinese surface-to-sea *Silkworm* missiles that it used during the Iran–Iraq War against Kuwaiti installations. As of the mid-1990s, Iran's cruise missile inventory consisted of HY-2 (*Silkworms*) and YJ-1 Chinese systems.

Iran has invested heavily in mine-warfare capabilities in the past several years. Many states have recognised their nuisance value in the confined and shallow waters of the Persian Gulf. During the last stages of the Iran–Iraq War, Iran laid close to 200 mines with the intention of disrupting the US naval operations and maritime traffic of the Arab Gulf states. Ten ships were hit by mines, including the US tanker, *Bridgeton*, and the USS *Samuel Roberts*. Mines are

small, cheap, easy to produce and lay, and create problems dispro-
portionate to the effort of laying them.[18]

Iran has laid the foundations for a submarine force with the
purchase of Russian-built *Kilo*-class submarines. The *Kilos* are
modern diesel-powered boats armed with 18 torpedoes, they carry a
sophisticated sonar system, and can lay up to 24 mines.[19] Submarines enhance prestige, but more important, they provide leverage
during wartime, forcing the naval units of major powers to spend an
inordinate amount of time and resources stalking them. Iran will
probably never master submarine warfare, but it has shown ingenu-
ity and skill in ensuring that its current fleet of two submarines
maintains operational readiness.[20]

Iran's strategic naval problem is one that weaker naval powers
have faced throughout history: how to deal with the might of vastly
more powerful navies. Iran is unlikely to implement a conventional
naval strategy against potential enemies like the US, despite its
sizeable conventional naval forces. It is more likely to adopt a naval
guerrilla strategy, or what has been traditionally called *une guerre
de course*, defined in Iran's case as raising the costs of Western
naval activity in the Persian Gulf. This would mean using a sea-
denial strategy designed initially to prevent the deployment of hostile forces in the Persian Gulf by sealing the Straits of Hormuz.

Revitalising Ground Forces
Iran's post-war priorities for ground forces included replacing
equipment lost in 1988, meeting current force-structure needs and
acquiring modern systems. It imported a modest quantity of artillery, tanks and armoured vehicles between 1989 and 1992. Iran is
also interested in acquiring more modern systems, and seeks sophisticated fire-control and target-acquisition systems for its artillery.

Iran is focusing on military reorganisation, intensive training
and the formulation of new doctrine in order to rectify severe
problems uncovered during the Iran–Iraq War. Recriminations
against those held responsible for military failures followed Iran's
severe defeats in spring and summer 1988. In May 1988, Brigadier-
General Ismail Sohrabi was dismissed as the armed forces chief-of-
staff. IRGC commander Mohsen Reza'i was publicly humiliated
when he was forced to admit to misappropriation of public funds and
to take responsibility for Iran's major setback at Faw in April. The
IRGC's strategy in the last stages of the war was severely criticised
in closed *Majlis* debates in late 1988. Guardsmen were accused of
mass desertion, corruption and of seeking easy jobs in Tehran.

But the harshest criticisms concerned the almost total lack of coordination between Iran's many forces that became evident in 1988. Iran's attempt to bring about more cohesion between the regular army and *Pasdaran* came in June when Rafsanjani was appointed acting Commander-in-Chief of the armed forces. Rafsanjani was tasked with establishing a general command headquarters; coordinating between all three forces; eliminating waste and duplication; consolidating the logistical capabilities of the armed forces; and combining the *Pasdar*'s military industries with those of the regular armed forces. Attempts from 1988 onwards to merge the regular army and the *Pasdars* were unsuccessful. Some government factions believed that such a combination would decrease the *Pasdars*' effectiveness in defending the Revolution. When the merger was debated within the *Majlis*, many members were wary of the potential dissolution of an important pillar of the Revolution.[21] Neither organisation was amenable to the idea, and the *Pasdaran*, a powerful political and socio-economic constituency, feared the loss of their privileges and status. The Iranian Army feared the dilution of its professionalism and technical skills, and being completely subsumed by the merger. But in 1992, a single office of the joint chiefs-of-staff was set up with the regular armed forces, thus eliminating separate command structures. The *Pasdars* have been forced to professionalise themselves by accepting a hierarchical rank structure like the regular army. They will continue to protect the internal security of the country, and provide the Iranian Army with support in the event of an attack by foreign forces. The Army is reorganising into a smaller, more professional force capable of conducting combined-arms warfare under all kinds of conditions, including chemical attack.[22] Its success depends on training intensity, the quality of army personnel and access to land-warfare weapons systems.

Organising Defence Industries
The development of Iran's defence-industrial infrastructure is a realistic aim because Iran has a 60-year-old defence base. The Shah had wanted to make Iran self-sufficient in certain areas of military production as part of his ambitious long-range industrialisation strategy. By 1979, the Iranian defence industries could assemble artillery pieces, small arms, large-calibre weapons, rockets and spare parts for armoured vehicles.[23]

The leaders of the Islamic Republic believe that the defence industries built by the Shah were too dependent on Western experts and technicians who were loathe to transfer any real technical skills to Iran. The Islamic Republic wants to build up an arms industry to protect its political, economic and military independence. The war with Iraq showed that Iran was indeed too dependent on outside suppliers for weapons systems and spare parts. Too often Iranian offensives were either postponed or failed because of inadequate arms and munitions supplies. Like other Middle Eastern states, Iran learned that a foreign supplier of arms is not reliable all the time, and may choose or be pressured to end the arms trade.

Despite frequent unsubstantiated claims that the Islamic Republic can produce major weapons systems, like main battle tanks, Iran's defence industries only currently ensure a measure of self-sufficiency in ammunition and light arms. Iran's medium-term goal is to build an industrial-military infrastructure closely tied to key sectors of the civilian industry. It will build components for weapons obtained from foreign suppliers, make major modifications to foreign weapons, and mass produce simple weapons based on indigenous designs. Faced with severe shortages of spares and components for its US-made equipment, Iran has developed a considerable capacity for modernisation and retrofit.

Developing an export market, a strategy that will lower production costs, will be difficult. Iran's defence industries have been plagued with duplication of efforts, tremendous waste, poor quality control, inadequate storage facilities and corruption. For a long time, the regular military and *Pasdars* had parallel but separate weapons-production efforts. The *Pasdar* enterprise (controlled by the IRGC Ministry) received a stinging critique in the *Majlis* in late 1988. When he was appointed Minister of Defence and Logistics in August 1989, Akbar Torkan moved to integrate these separate efforts.

If the arms industry is to become efficient and more technically sophisticated, it will require substantial investment. It also needs to devote more resources to research and development. Iranian R&D funding and manpower levels are well below global standards. Iran lacks a sufficient technical, scientific and engineering cadre; thousands of qualified professionals fled the country taking valuable skills with them. The educational system is in decay, not only because of the migration of academics, but also because of the state's cultural revolution and its efforts to make the educational system more Islamic.[24]

Iran's research centres and educational institutions are substandard, archaic and ridden with bureaucracy. There is no culture of research and researchers are poorly trained. Institutions of higher learning suffer from inadequate funding; one Iranian described, 'the libraries of many of the universities in Iran do not comply with world and academic standards, and the existing resources are in some cases old and unusable'.[25] Improving education requires expanding R&D, obtaining more books, equipment and publications from abroad, and establishing contact with international scientific circles.

Iran and Weapons of Mass Destruction

The Iran–Iraq War was the first Middle East war to see large-scale use of both chemical weapons and ballistic missiles. The changes that WMD had created in the strategic environment worried the Iranians.[26] Little is known about the present Iranian chemical weapons programme. In early 1993, Iran signed the Chemical Weapons Convention calling for the prohibition of the development, production, stockpiling and use of chemical weapons. This action may indicate Iran's desire to expend scarce resources on two more effective WMD, ballistic missiles and nuclear weapons. It is Iran's investment in a ballistic-missile capability and in nuclear weapons that has caused the most concern in the international community.

Iran's Ballistic-Missile Programme

Iran has shown no reticence about its possession of ballistic missiles. President Rafsanjani himself has repeatedly indicated that Iran has a powerful ballistic-missile capability. Yet, this may be wishful thinking. Iran's indigenous efforts in this field have been plagued by technical problems, but it is clear that Iran would like to have a powerful ballistic-missile deterrent force. This stems from its experiences during the war with Iraq and its perceptions of the impact of Iraq's use of ballistic missiles during the Gulf War.

Iraq used ballistic missiles and rockets from the beginning of the Iran–Iraq War and urban areas in Iran suffered severely. But it was the war of the cities in February–March 1988 that traumatised the Iranians most. Iraq launched almost 200 missiles at Tehran, Isfahan and Qom, causing 2,000 Iranian deaths, 8,000 injuries and considerable property damage. The attacks prompted mass terror and hundreds of thousands of Tehran residents fled the city, highlighting the lack of effective defence or deterrent.[27]

Iran had considerably exaggerated its own capabilities in the mid-1980s, and despite its ability to target Baghdad, it could not sustain a prolonged missile offensive nor retaliate on a one-to-one basis during the ferocious war of the cities. This humiliating situation fuelled Iran's attempts to develop and acquire long-range ballistic missiles as a future deterrent or retaliatory capability.

Iran's desire to acquire ballistic missiles in the aftermath of the Iran–Iraq War was primarily motivated by Iraqi developments in the field and by a general proliferation of ballistic missiles in Middle East states. Saudi Arabia, Pakistan, Afghanistan, Syria and Israel are all known to have ballistic missiles, though Iraq remains the focus of concern. The Iranians suspected as early as 1988 that the Iraqis were capable of putting chemical warheads on their ballistic missiles.

Since 1994, Iran's ballistic-missile programme has come from two separate but interrelated initiatives.[28] First, Iran has openly purchased missiles from North Korea, China, Libya and Syria. It obtained *Scuds* from Libya in 1985 and from Syria in 1986 to retaliate during the war with Iraq. Second, since 1985 when it decided to invest in an indigenous ballistic-missile capability, Iran has sought assistance from North Korea and China.

North Korea assisted Iran with the *Scud* series missiles following a 1985 agreement to transfer manufacturing know-how for SAMs. This technology transfer reportedly helped Iran with the production of its indigenous series of artillery rockets and the construction of a production facility for the *Scud*-B. In early 1990, Iran received 100–200 missiles from North Korea and further assistance in setting-up missile-production facilities and training Iranians in the manufacture, deployment and testing of ballistic missiles. It was reported that some of the missiles were *Scud*-Cs acquired to provide the basis for an indigenous *Scud*-C programme. (The C-series missile is more accurate than the *Scud*-B, has twice the range and carries a warhead three times more powerful.) In early 1992, it was reported (but is, as yet, unconfirmed) that Iran and North Korea were cooperating to produce the long-range liquid-propelled *No Dong*-1 missile that would carry a 1,760 pound conventional warhead. This missile would be more powerful than anything currently in Iran's arsenal.

Iran could be collaborating with other Third World states. In late 1991, it was reported that Iran and Syria – *de facto* allies since the early 1980s – had agreed to pool their resources to develop ballistic missiles.[29] Other reports suggest that Iran had approached other countries like Brazil – which had helped Iraq with ballistic-missile and artillery rocket systems – for missile technology. Iran could possibly collaborate with Brazil, which is rapidly becoming one of the leading Third World ballistic-missile producers.

Iran was impressed by the psychological impact and urban damage caused by ballistic missiles in Israel during the Gulf War, and by the inordinate amount of time coalition jets spent looking unsuccessfully for *Scud* launchers. After the Gulf War, Iranian commentators urged more investment in short-, medium- and long-range surface-to-surface missiles to deter enemy strikes against economic and urban centres. In January 1991, Tehran announced that it would start mass-producing long-range surface-to-surface missiles with great destructive power.[30]

Iran's production of ballistic missiles, as opposed to primitive unguided rockets, will not be an easy task. Reports indicate that there are tremendous 'bottlenecks' throughout Iran's indigenous ballistic-missile production programme, and shortages of skilled personnel, technology and materials.[31]

Iran's Nuclear Programme

It is the nuclear aspect of Iran's rearmament programme that has caused the most controversy and alarm in the past five years. However, there are two sets of views concerning the status of Iran's nuclear capabilities. The Central Intelligence Agency and Western defence analysts have argued since the early 1990s that it will take 8–10 years before Iran has a nuclear capability. Yet, in January 1995, even more alarmist assessments emerged from the United States and Israel.

The other view emphasises the obstacles Iran faces in acquiring a nuclear capability, but does not doubt Iran's intention to acquire them. The Russian Foreign Intelligence Service believes that due to Iran's weakened condition, the underdevelopment of the industrial and scientific base, and investment requirements of $1–1.5bn annually, it is unlikely that the Islamic Republic will acquire nuclear weapons any time soon.

Because of its predecessor's interest in the development of Iran's nuclear infrastructure, the Islamic Republic inherited a large technical nuclear base. Imperial Iran had extensive plans in the civilian nuclear field, having argued that it needed civilian nuclear power because its oil reserves were limited. In 1957, Iran signed an agreement with the United States to cooperate in the peaceful use of nuclear energy, and in 1970, Iran signed the Nuclear Non-Proliferation Treaty (NPT). Like its neighbour Iraq, Iran had sent thousands of students and technicians to the West to study nuclear physics and receive advanced training. In 1974, it lent its support to a call to make the Middle East a WMD-free zone. The same year, the Shah established the Atomic Energy Organisation of Iran (AEOI) and began the most ambitious commercial nuclear energy programme in the Middle East, which would have provided Iran with 23 nuclear power stations by the mid-1990s. In 1976, the Federal Republic of Germany agreed to build two 1,300MW plants at Bushehr, which were 60% and 75% complete when the Shah fell from power. In January 1995, when Iran reached an accord with Russia to complete its nuclear reactors at Bushehr, Tehran found itself embroiled in another controversy it could ill afford: speculation about the Islamic Republic's nuclear intentions and capabilities.

Non-proliferation analysts were divided on whether imperial Iran had a clandestine nuclear-weapons programme. In the 1970s, Alvin Cottrell, a US analyst sympathetic to the Shah, dismissed speculations about Iranian nuclear-military ambitions as 'premature and exaggerated'.[32] Iran was a signatory of the NPT and a fervent advocate of a nuclear-free Middle East. Although the Shah stated that he had no intention of acquiring nuclear weapons, he made it very clear that Iran's non-acquisition of such weapons depended on the extent of non-proliferation in the region; he told Egyptian journalist Mohammed Hasanein Heykal, 'Iran will have to acquire atomic bombs if some upstart in the region gets them'.[33]

Between 1979 and 1984, Iran's nuclear programme collapsed because of the post-Revolution chaos, a preoccupation with the war with Iraq, the flight of thousands of Iranian technical experts and scientists from Iran, and disorganisation of higher education. The Islamic Republic conceded that this period was a low-point in the development of the AEOI, which lost much of its financing and half its personnel, either through transfer or emigration.[34] Low-level nuclear research continued at the Tehran Research Center using a small research reactor, and a nuclear research centre at the University of Isfahan opened in 1984.[35]

The Russian Federation Foreign Intelligence Service Report on WMD proliferation pointed out that there has been a rise in cooperation between 'threshold' and 'near-threshold' powers.[36] It was in the mid-1980s that Iran began seeking nuclear cooperation with countries that had nuclear expertise. In 1986, Pakistan reportedly offered to train Iranian scientists in return for financial assistance with Pakistan's own nuclear programme, and in 1987, both countries signed an agreement on technical cooperation in the military-nuclear field that included dispatching 39 Iranian nuclear scientists to Pakistan for training.[37] Pakistani–Iranian cooperation may have deepened after the visit to Pakistan of the Iranian Speaker of the

Majlis in February 1991. Rumours notwithstanding, Pakistan is unlikely to give Iran an atomic device or a workable weapons design. It does not wish to border yet another nuclear power; but more importantly, it would seriously damage Islamabad's relations with the West. Pakistan will probably limit itself to training Iranian scientists and engineers. But like Iraq, Iran could learn a great deal from Pakistan's programme for the procurement of dual-use technologies and the pitfalls of developing a nuclear capability.

In 1987, Iran signed an agreement with Argentina to supply enriched uranium to the small Tehran research reactor, and train Iranian scientists at an Argentinian nuclear centre. Efforts to acquire nuclear-related technology appear to have gathered momentum after a February 1987 AEOI meeting with then President Ali Khamene'i who allegedly called upon Iran's scientists to 'work hard and at great speed' to obtain atomic energy for Iran.[38] After the war with Iraq ended in 1988, Iran issued a call for the return of exiled scientists and technicians to help in the reconstruction of the country.

Iran has solicited assistance building a nuclear infrastructure from countries with advanced nuclear technology. Some of Iran's efforts have been stymied by reluctance to supply nuclear-related technology to a country suspected of an illegal weapons programme. Iran attempted to purchase German nuclear technology transferred to Brazil in the mid-1970s. Both the United States and Germany, as well as the Brazilian Foreign Ministry (which does not want Brazil to be blacklisted as a source of proliferation), objected to the proposed sale. Iran has also tried unsuccessfully to push Germany into finishing the reactors at Bushehr, severely damaged by the Iraqi Air Force on three separate occasions during the Iran–Iraq War.[39] Germany's refusal to finish the project has angered Iran considerably. A tremendous amount of money has already been sunk and its completion would signal post-war reconstruction success.

But two countries, namely China and Russia, have been willing to supply Iran with nuclear technology and training, and have not responded to Western pressure not to. China has supplied Iran with a variety of weapons systems and assistance with its ballistic-missile programme. However, the Sino–Iranian nuclear relationship has aroused the most concern in the 1990s.[40] A 1991 agreement to sell Iran a small 27KW research reactor seems to have been deferred. In 1992, the two signed an extensive scientific, technical and economic cooperation agreement including assistance in the construction of a safeguarded 300MW reactor, which has also been delayed. China's sale of an electromagnetic isotope separator (EMIS), or calutron – an antiquated process for separating the weapons-grade uranium-235 isotope from naturally occurring uranium-238 – generated considerable unease. An inefficient and obsolete method, the EMIS process recently gained notoriety because of the discovery after the Gulf War of Iraq's massive calutron-based enrichment installations at Tarmiya. However, the process is time-consuming and requires an extensive infrastructure and a staff of thousands. At this stage, Iran cannot use the EMIS process for uranium enrichment. The calutron supplied by the Chinese is small and is used solely for medical research.

Motivations and Incentives to Nuclearisation
Iran's motivations for acquiring nuclear weapons are numerous. Possession of nuclear weapons promises enhanced prestige and regional status. Iran's neighbour, Pakistan, is much poorer – in 1992 it ranked 120th out of 160 countries in overall human development, and 30% of its population lives below the poverty line – yet Pakistan is one of few nuclear states. With this exclusivity comes prestige and status.

Iran's acquisition of nuclear weapons would have both strategic and political value, providing deterrence against nuclear threats and intimidation by other states. Nuclear weapons could reduce the military options of 'global arrogance' – those of the United States and its allies – in the region. Iran is worried by the extent to which the United States has been able to influence world affairs, reinforced with modern and sophisticated conventional-weapons systems Iran has no chance of acquiring.

Paradoxically, while the utility of nuclear weapons has been de-emphasised by the West in the post-Cold War period in favour of reliance on sophisticated conventional technology, countries like Iran and North Korea might see nuclear weapons as the only way to deter the West. US conventional military strength may be an incentive for certain states to proliferate.

Iran claims to be concerned by the nuclearisation of the Middle East, which has proceeded apace since the mid-1970s. Iraq's incipient nuclearisation, uncovered by the UN in the wake of the Gulf War, shook Iran, which is aware that what Iraq has learned can never be unlearned. Coupled with Iran's respect for the Iraqi capacity for regeneration, Iran's reasons to fear the potential of Iraq's residual capabilities in the nuclear field continue to grow.

Ensuring a regional nuclear balance between Israel and the Islamic world might be another Iranian motivation to 'go nuclear'.

Iran could argue that the Arab failure to acquire a nuclear capability makes it the responsibility of the 'wider Islamic world' to do so. This line of thinking was espoused by Deputy President Ata'ollah Mohajerani who has stated on a number of occasions that if Israel continues to have nuclear arms, the Muslim states should cooperate to arm themselves with nuclear weapons. Otherwise, he asserted, Israel would use its weapons to maintain regional superiority. The only alternative to further regional nuclearisation, he argued, is to deprive the Israelis of such weapons (and Mohajerani's tough rhetoric indicates that he believes Israeli denuclearisation to be unlikely).[41] But the media and policy-makers outside Iran have made too much of this stance. It is highly unlikely that Iran would openly signal its desire to acquire nuclear weapons, nor must Mohajerani's views be taken as indicative of official views or policy. Mohajerani's statements were more likely made to assess popular reaction to them.

A nuclear programme is highly dependent on a government's ability to reach a consensus on the need for nuclearisation, and to be able to organise and manage a long-term complex project involving the coordination of state, scientific and technical infrastructure.

Since the decision to implement a nuclear-weapons programme is a secret one, it is difficult to ascertain whether, and if so when, the Iranian government took such a step. The positions of the various factions within the political establishment and the military are equally inscrutable. This is not to imply that an Iranian decision to acquire a nuclear capability would be subject to fierce debates within the *Majlis*. Rather, it would be undertaken *in camera* within the SNSC. But even decision-making in the SNSC may be hostage to factional interests. Since the clerical leadership is not monolithic, a cleric who might drum up evidence that nuclear weapons are consistent with Islam might be opposed by another arguing that they go against Islamic teachings on the conduct of war. Furthermore, the Revolutionary Guards might be the most averse to the acquisition of a weapons system that makes a mockery of their conception of a popular revolutionary war. However, if they were to retain command and control of Iran's nuclear-weapons stock they might adopt a different stance.

It is difficult to ascertain the motives of the various political factions. Concerned by the seemingly rampant global 'arrogance' of the United States, the radicals might argue that nuclear weapons would defend against American 'bullying habits'. The conservatives might also endorse such a view. The technocrats would be the greatest supporters of a covert nuclear programme because of the relatively low cost of nuclear weapons compared to a conventional acquisition programme. The technocrats, who see technology as a panacea and focus on rational decision-making in a period of economic hardship, might also support a nuclear solution to Iran's defence dilemma. If the technocrats and their clerical allies, like President Rafsanjani, set Iran on a course of acquiring a nuclear-weapons capability, the political and economic links they seek with the outside world will be threatened. Indeed, the suspicion in the West that Iran is actually aspiring to attain a nuclear capability is yet one more issue that perpetuates Iran's negative image, and may lead to the kind of economic and political pressure that the United States would like to see imposed on Iran.

Obstacles and Disincentives to Nuclearisation
The greatest obstacle to Iranian nuclearisation is the acquisition of fissile material, either highly enriched uranium or separated plutonium. To make an atomic bomb from uranium-235, naturally occurring uranium-238 must be upgraded at an enrichment plant using one or more of the following methods: gaseous diffusion, gas centrifuges, calutrons, aerodynamic separation, chemical enrichment or laser enrichment, all of which require large installations, costly equipment and many technicians and scientists. Apart from the unclassified calutron method, which Iraq had used, uranium-enrichment technology is not widely available. Secret facilities would require dual-use technologies and high-precision machine tools that careful monitoring could detect, particularly if the country in question is suspected of wanting nuclear weapons – and Iran is. Iran has no known uranium-enrichment facilities, although it is suspected of building a centrifuge-enrichment facility at Karaj, north of Tehran. The expense, difficulty of gaining access to classified enrichment technologies, and the need for a large, skilled technical base has meant that the enriched-uranium route has traditionally been passed over in favour of the plutonium route, using a nuclear reactor. A small nuclear reactor and a primitive reprocessing facility to produce plutonium and recover it from irradiated reactor fuel would require a modest technological infrastructure and hundreds of millions of dollars.[42] But Iran does not currently have either a reactor or a reprocessing facility capable of producing weapons-grade plutonium.

Fissile material can be purchased. Enriched uranium or plutonium from the former Soviet Union could feasibly find its way to the Middle East. Security at Russian nuclear installations is notable for its absence, and there are growing fears that organised crime in Russia is setting up a nuclear smuggling infrastructure.[43] Iran and Iraq are clearly suspected of being potential fissile-material customers. After many false starts and embarrassing failures, Iran developed a covert procurement network during the Iran–Iraq War dedicated to the acquisition of arms and spare parts. What is of concern to the outside world is that such a network has branched out into dual-technology acquisition and may have been assisted by Pakistani and Iraqi networks in the West.

The acquisition of fissile material is only one in a series of hurdles Iran faces in attaining a nuclear capability, but it is the hardest to leap. No nuclear-weapons programme has ever succeeded without a coalition of high politics and grand science. Intense political factionalism in the Islamic Republic limits its ability to maintain the direction and coordination necessary for a nuclear-weapons programme. Such factionalism is deeply embedded in the political structure and had a very negative impact on the war effort against Iraq and the formulation of domestic and foreign policy agendas. It would be facile to assume that Tehran speaks with one voice on the issue of nuclearisation, as the Central Intelligence Agency and the Defense Intelligence Agency are wont to believe.

Iran also faces severe structural problems. Its technical infrastructure is inadequate and its personnel demoralised. The structural problems in the defence industries will also hinder the nuclear programme.

Controversy over the Nuclear Programme
The revelation of Iraq's enormous nuclear programme by the UN 'Special Commission' (UNSCOM) has led analysts and officials outside Iran to err on the side of caution and to argue that Iran's ultimate goal is to attain nuclear weapons. A visit by the International Atomic Energy Agency to Iranian nuclear installations in early 1992, which gave Iran a 'clean bill of health', should not be construed as proof that Iran is not working on acquiring nuclear weapons. The Iranians only took the inspectors to sites of Iran's choosing. Iran, unlike Iraq, is not subject to international sanctions and inspections.

Iran, naturally, has vehemently denied that it is seeking to acquire nuclear weapons. It is conceivable that the Iranian leadership's denials are part of a sophisticated dissimulation strategy to deflect attention away from any putative nuclearisation efforts.

Iranian newspapers and officials attacked the United States for arrogating to itself the right unilaterally to decide who can and cannot have nuclear technology.[44] Islamic states, the reports contend, have an unequivocal right to acquire nuclear weapons if they so chose, even though, as is the case with Iran, they might not exercise it. Yet some Iranian officials and military officers have stated that it would be politically unwise for Iran to acquire nuclear weapons. Moral values based on Islamic principles, they argue, preclude the acquisition of such weapons; nor does Iran's defence strategy, based on its people's faith, courage and experience derived from the Iran–Iraq War, require nuclear weapons.[45] Nuclear weapons, they continue, have not proven their usefulness in the contemporary world: they are militarily useless and financially ruinous.[46] Even if Iran were to acquire them, the argument follows, it would still face states with vastly more powerful atomic arsenals.[47] Iran's official position is that it seeks ultimately to bring about the global de-legitimisation of nuclear weapons and to prevent horizontal and vertical proliferation in accordance with the NPT.[48]

Iran intends and believes it has the right to acquire nuclear power for peaceful civilian purposes.[49] The Islamic Republic rejects the argument that because it is an oil-rich country it does not need to invest in nuclear power as an alternative energy source. Oil reserves, Iranian officials argue, will not last forever, and if Iran does not keep abreast of current developments in the nuclear field it will fall far behind the rest of the world.[50]

Iran could be following in the footsteps of covert proliferants like India, Pakistan, Israel and Iraq, each of which always denied – particularly in the initial stages of their nuclear programmes – any intention of producing nuclear weapons. It is politically unwise for a would-be proliferant to claim that its nuclear programme is designed to produce atomic bombs because of the political, moral and economic pressure that could be exerted by powerful anti-proliferation groups, and because of the risk of military attack. Iran would have every reason to camouflage its own activities in light of recent Israeli claims that the nuclearisation of Iran – or of any hostile state – is a threat to it. Iran is well aware that in order to maintain its unilateral nuclear capability, Israel has resorted to sabotage, air strikes, assassinations and air strikes against Arab, especially Iraqi sites.[51] In the aftermath of the Gulf War and the discovery of Iraq's massive nuclear-weapons programme, Iran and any other would-be proliferant is unlikely to give any state the excuse to engage in 'coercive disarmament'. Rather, these proliferants would adopt a long-term, incremental and covert strategy of building the required infrastructure. Like Iraq, Iran could be building infrastructure underground in protected and camouflaged sites.[52]

The perception that the Islamic Republic is pursuing a nuclear capability is yet another factor perpetuating the country's negative image, with potentially serious national-security implications. Fearful of Iranian pretensions, the Israelis have taken the lead since the early 1990s in sounding the alarm over Iran's presumed nuclear programme. This response ties in with Israel's perception of the Islamic Republic as a dire threat to peace and order in the Middle East because of its support for Islamists and its opposition to the peace process.[53] The Israelis may have also wished to exaggerate the matter in order to press the United States and the West to take a more active approach.[54] Israel itself has raised the ante *vis-à-vis* Iran – which it now regards as a serious antagonist – and has stated that if the international community is unable to exert political pressure to stop Iran, it could become an Israeli target.[55] In 1981, the Israeli Air Force destroyed Iraq's nuclear reactor at Osirak. The Iranians have since warned that Israel would pay a 'heavy price' for any attack.[56] Nevertheless, it is plausible that the Israelis would strike at Iranian infrastructure it suspects of furthering Iran's nuclear aspirations.

Iran's activities in the nuclear field and the agreement reached in early 1995 with Russia to finish the Bushehr reactors have led to a renewed focus on the Islamic Republic's intentions. At the same time reports appeared in both the United States and Israel that Iran was only five to seven years away from an indigenously developed and deployed nuclear capability. There was no proof for the assertion, though it suspiciously coincided with US Secretary of Defense William Perry's extensive visit to the Middle East and South Asia in April 1995 to highlight the dangers of nuclear proliferation and muster support for indefinite extension of the NPT. Furthermore, the controversy over Iran's nuclear programme also coincides with the growing perception in Israel and the United States that the Islamic Republic is a serious threat to global peace and stability. Ironically, in view of the differences between them, both Arabs and Iranians have discovered common ground in the belief that the early 1995 controversy over Iran's Islamic bomb was an attempt to deflect attention from the fact that in the mid-1990s Israel is the only nuclear power in the Middle East, a source of anxiety to both Arabs and Iranians.

The Islamic Republic of Iran faces a daunting task in its quest to reconstruct Iranian military power. It does not have the financial resources to engage in a massive, across-the-board modernisation and acquisition programme for its conventional forces. It is striving to maintain ageing systems for as long as possible. Its ground forces have taken second place to the acquisition and modernisation programmes of Iran's Air Force, air defences and Navy. It is in these three areas that the Islamic Republic feels most threatened by outside powers and feels that it can build an adequate defensive, deterrent and offensive capability. The Islamic Republic currently does not fear a serious ground threat from any of its neighbours, including Iraq. Its ground forces are still beset by severe organisational, command and coordination problems, and it is unlikely that these will be fully resolved unless or until the Iranians overcome intense factionalism within the political system. The problems associated with nuclearisation and the obstacles facing Iran's nuclear programme may impel the leadership to find a short-term solution in developing radiological weapons, 'dirty bombs', which consist of fissile material enriched to a low level, but are deadly enough to be an adequate deterrent and retaliatory threat.

Iran has clearly not yet developed a nuclear-weapons capability and reports of secret nuclear sites being built are unsubstantiated. Reports in the early 1990s that Iran had acquired 3–5 tactical nuclear weapons or components from Kazakhstan turned out to be false.

In the final analysis, Iran's nuclear-weapons development programme would not be the massive, sophisticated, expensive and multi-pronged uranium-enrichment programme that Iraq's was. Iran does not currently have the financial resources nor the scientific and technical infrastructure for such a programme, nor does it need one to become a significant nuclear state.

CONCLUSION

With its economy in free-fall, growing popular alienation, a political system facing a crisis of legitimacy, and problems with the outside world, the Islamic Republic of Iran is at a crossroads. There was little cause for celebration during the sixteenth anniversary of the Islamic Revolution in February 1995. The economy is stagnant and severely burdened with debt repayments to foreign creditors – a source of extreme humiliation – that consume almost $8bn annually, over half the country's oil revenue.

Whether it survives the crisis is open to question. The 'Panglossian' optimism of a number of Iranian technocrats – who foresee Iran successfully meeting its obligations to its creditors in the short term, and transforming into an economic powerhouse in the long term – is not universally shared. Even the clerics are increasingly worried.

The policies of the second republic are in shambles and its supporters in disarray. It has been difficult for Rafsanjani to convince the clerical elite that reforms are essential to the survival of the system. The clerics recognise the necessity of reforms, but dare not carry them out because they do not want to reform themselves out of existence. It is unlikely that the second republic will see a turnaround before mid-1997 when Rafsanjani's second and final presidential term expires. What, then, does the future hold? The Islamic Republic could continue to 'muddle through', lurching from crisis to crisis, hoping to find *ad hoc* solutions to its political and socio-economic problems. This situation, in any case, is likely to characterise the twilight years of the Rafsanjani presidency. With respect to foreign policy, its primary strategy will be to stave off any political and economic pressures from the West, particularly the United States. The Islamic Republic's negative image in the West has not substantially improved. On the contrary, Iran's support for Islamist movements and opposition to the Arab–Israeli peace process, both core legitimising elements of its ideology, are obstacles to improved relations. Iran's perceived quest for nuclear weapons contributes to suspicion of it. The Islamic Republic has adroitly managed to avoid pressures designed to change its behaviour; but it is walking a tightrope. It is more susceptible to the vagaries of the international economic system than at any other time in its history. Any terrorist act linked to Iran or incontrovertible evidence that it is seeking a nuclear-weapons capability may bring about concerted Western pressure to stop it.

Domestic politics will determine whether the clerics will stand or fall. To their credit, the clerics recognise that the United States and the West cannot be blamed for all that has gone wrong in Iran – either in the last 16 years or in the past several decades. In this context, the presidential elections of 1997 will be of crucial importance, particularly with respect to the religious nature of the regime as well as its evolution. The issue of whether the Constitution will be amended to allow Rafsanjani to run for a third term has already been raised by one of the President's advisors, Ata'ollah Mohajerani.[1] It was quickly shot down in the *Majlis* ostensibly for fear of institutionalising a 'dictatorial presidency', but more for fear of pushing Rafsanjani out of this office.

Potential aspirants to the presidency include *Hojjatolislam* Ali Akbar Nateq Nuri, the Speaker of the *Majlis*, and *Hojjatolislam* Hasan Ruhani, Rafsanjani's adviser at the SNSC. In 1994, a senior cleric, Ayatollah Mahdavi-Kani, caused a stir when he suggested that clerics should not run for president in 1997. Among the non-clerics who could aspire to the presidency, two possible candidates stand out.[2] One is the tough, no-nonsense technocratic mayor of Tehran, Gholam Hossein Karbatschi, who has achieved the impossible by improving municipal efficiency. Karbatschi, however, has not shown an interest in running for the presidency. Another potential candidate is the powerful Minister of the Interior, Ali Mohammed Besharati, a high-profile conservative protégé of Ayatollah Khamene'i. His mandate as Interior Minister and chief of the internal security services, and his conservative ideological outlook have conditioned a tough approach to combating 'social corruption', urban violence and narcotics, though he holds liberal beliefs about the formation of political parties. Besharati's reputation and influence hinge on the political fortunes of Ayatollah Khamene'i. Whether a Besharati presidency, or indeed any president, can revitalise the economy, stabilise Iran's relations with the outside world and implement political reforms is open to question.

A 'corrective revolution' by radicals or hardliners is also possible. A radical regime would put renewed emphasis on distributive economic policies and social justice. It would retain much of Khomeini's foreign-policy legacy with its pronounced opposition to the forces of 'global arrogance'. But a radical corrective revolution is unlikely. Unlike the plotters of the August 1991 coup in the Soviet Union who suffered from a 'mythic nostalgia' for the normality represented by the communist past, the radicals in Iran cannot point to such an 'idyll'.[3] The first decade of the Islamic Republic was one of bloody revolution, war and consolidation of power; its leaders are still unable to show what the benefits of the revolutionary decade were. The radicals are divided, and their statist economic policies dated. Their constituency – the dispossessed – is spiritually exhausted, impatient and more impoverished than ever. Furthermore, there is a profound psychological need for predictability in everyday life, sorely lacking in the 16 years of the Islamic Republic.

The conservative Islamic right, whose power has risen since its *Majlis* victory in 1992, is likely to make a political shift towards the interests of the *bazaaris*. Subsidies and price controls will be 'thrown' to the lower classes to avoid greater social distress and mass discontent. The conservatives' social and cultural agenda is evident in their frantic efforts to thwart the West's 'cultural assault' on the Islamic Republic. Nothing illustrates this better than the fierce *Majlis* debates on banning satellite dishes which beam in 'filthy' Western programmes allegedly undermining the social and cultural fabric of the country and corrupting 'homo Islamicus'. But a conservative Islamic Iran will be caught in a paradoxical situation: while it may derive legitimacy from the groundswell of Islamic movements in the Middle East, domestically it is facing a popular nationalist backlash against stultifying Islamic culture.

The demise of the Islamic Republic is not an impossibility. The considerable resources that Middle East states have historically brought to bear to preserve the power of the elite should not be underestimated. In the case of the Islamic Republic, however, the combination of political and socio-economic problems and the moral crisis may be too much for the regime to endure. A confluence of incidents could destabilise the Islamic Republic, and the system might spontaneously explode.

But a revolution is not a certainty either. Iranians are politically cynical after years of revolutionary mobilisation, and an ideological alternative does not exist (at least not openly). The lack of a credible mass-based alternative ensures legitimacy by default, and thus the tenuous survival of the clerical regime – hardly a source of satisfaction for the clerics.

Iranians are also afraid of substituting one ideological system for another. The vibrant intellectual and academic debate taking place out of government control is a manifestation of the widening cleavage between the state and civil society. It is also an indication of frustration with an ideological system that sees itself as the sole repository of truth.

As Tehran finds it increasingly difficult to fund development in the provinces, Iran could decentralise.[4] Turmoil in peripheral regions may further stretch the resources of internal security forces. At this point, an armed-forces intervention, or lack thereof, would be a critical variable in the evolution of the political process. If provincial garrisons refuse to intervene to shore up the centre's collapsing authority, it would accelerate decentralisation.

The military could intervene, either to shore up the clerical regime by putting down mass insurrections, or to remove it. The possibility of a 'man on horseback' taking power cannot be excluded either. Iranian history has two examples of military leaders stepping into politics to reverse Iran's decline: Nader Shah in the eighteenth century; and Reza Shah in the twentieth. The armed forces – both regular and revolutionary – have been under stringent political and ideological control, but they are increasingly dissatisfied. This dissatisfaction could manifest itself in overt opposition to the clerical regime.

The Islamic Republic no longer has the ability to draw up or implement domestic or foreign policies that would lead to the emergence of a flourishing and vibrant society and an economy worthy of emulation by the rest of the Muslim world. Unless it gains renewed confidence that could stave off looming disaster (from something as mundane as a dramatic rise in oil prices or from the sudden downfall of a secular Arab regime), the days when the Islamic Revolution could have a meaningful impact are over.

73

Notes

Introduction
[1] See James Wyllie, 'Iran – The Edge of the Precipice', *Jane's Intelligence Review*, vol. 6, no. 4, April 1994, pp. 176–77; Thierry Lalevée, 'L'Iran en voie d'implosion?', *Arabies*, no. 74, February 1993, pp. 18–27; *New York Times*, 20 November 1994; 'Iran: An Economy in Disarray', *The Middle East*, December 1994; and two excellent articles by Robin Wright, *Los Angeles Times*, 2 and 13 December 1994.

[2] For a vehemently ideological example of this view, see James Philips, 'The Saddamization of Iran', *Policy Review*, no. 69, Summer 1994, pp. 6–13. For a more measured analysis see, Ephraim Kam, 'The Iranian Threat', in Shlomo Gazit and Zeev Eytan, *The Middle East Military Balance 1993–1994* (Jerusalem and Boulder, CO: Jerusalem Post and Westview Press for the Jaffee Center for Strategic Studies, 1994), pp. 73–90.

[3] The term 'second republic' was first used by Anoushiravan Ehteshami, an Iran specialist at the University of Durham. See his new book, *After Khomeini: The Iranian Second Republic* (London: Routledge, 1995).

[4] For further analysis, see David Armstrong, *Revolution and World Order: The Revolutionary State in International Society* (Oxford: Clarendon Press, 1993).

[5] I am indebted to Dr Ahmad Salmatian for these figures, 19 April 1994, Paris.

Chapter I
[1] Jamshid Amuzegar, *Iran's Economy under The Islamic Republic* (London: I. B. Tauris, 1993), p. 312.

[2] Shahrough Akhavi, 'Elite Factionalism in the Islamic Republic of Iran', *Middle East Journal*, vol. 41, no. 2, Spring 1987, p. 182; David Menashri, 'The Clerical Power Struggle and the Fourth Majlis Elections', *Orient*, vol. 33, no. 3, 1992, pp. 377–408.

[3] Ahmad Salamatian, 'L'Imam Khomeini Contre les Conservateurs', *Le Monde Diplomatique*, June 1988, p. 14.

[4] What follows is a highly simplified categorisation of these political factional differences. For a detailed and succinct overview, see Patrick Clawson, 'Iran's Challenge to the West: How, When and Why', Washington Institute for Near East Policy, Paper no. 33, 1993, pp. 5–27.

[5] Quoted in David Hirst, *The Guardian*, 16 July 1981.

[6] *New York Times*, 31 January 1993.

[7] Amuzegar, *Iran's Economy under the Islamic Republic*, p. 32.

[8] Quoted in *Tehran Times*, 19 September 1982, p. 1.

[9] *Foreign Broadcast Information Service* (*FBIS*)-NEA, 29 July 1990, p. 57.

[10] Ahmad Salamatian, 'La Révolution Iranienne Broyé par ses Contradictions', *Le Monde Diplomatique*, 20 June 1993.

[11] *BBC Summary of World Broadcasts* (*SWB*), ME/2085, 27 August 1994, p. S/1/1.

[12] Chris Kutschera, 'Iran's Peeling Veneer', *The Middle East*, September 1994, p. 20; *International Herald Tribune*, 6 July 1994, pp. 1 and 4.

[13] As defined by Felix Rohatyn, 'World Capital: The Need and the Risks', *New York Review of Books*, 14 July 1994, p. 49.

[14] See *Gulf States Newsletter*, no. 414, 1 July 1991, p. 9.

[15] See *Al-Majallah*, 6 November 1994, pp. 26–28.

[16] See *SWB*, MEW/0330, 26 April 1994, WME/2-WME/6.

[17] *SWB*, 27 August 1994, ME/2085 S1/11.

[18] See *Middle East Economic Digest*, 30 September 1994, p. 12.

[19] *The Echo of Iran*, no. 69, November 1993, p. 13.

[20] This constituency is well described in Shireen Hunter, *Iran After Khomeini*, Washington Paper No. 156 (Washington DC: Center for Strategic and International Studies, 1992), p. 43.

[21] Amir Taheri, 'Téhéran: Le Thermidor Avorté', *Politique Internationale*, no. 64, Summer 1994, p. 147.

[22] 'Iran: La Faction Radicale aux Commandes', *Arabies*, no. 87, March 1994, p. 7.

[23] *Middle East Monitor*, February 1994, p. 11.

[24] *Gulf States Newsletter*, no. 414, 1 July 1991, p. 10.

[25] *SWB*, 14 June 1993, ME/1714/A/5.

[26] See *SWB*, ME/1898, 18 January 1994, p. MED/11.

[27] For succinct analyses of the origins of and problems posed by Ayatollah Khomeini's theory of government, see Hunter, *Iran After Khomeini*, pp. 14–28; and Shaul Bakhash, 'Iran: The Crisis of Legitimacy' (unpublished paper).

[28] This section is based largely on the following sources: Johannes Riessner, *Teheran und Washington: Auf dem Weg zur Normalisierung?* (*Tehran and Washington: On the Road to Normalisation?*) (Ebenhausen: Stiftung Wissenschaft und Politik, 1994), pp. 17–19; Bakhash, 'Iran: The Crisis of Legitimacy', pp. 13–21; W. G. Milward, 'Political Dimensions of the Marja'iyate in Ithna'ashari Shi'ism: Recent Devlopments', paper presented at the Twenty-eighth Annual Meeting of the Middle East Studies Association, Phoenix, AZ, 19–22 November 1994, pp. 15–19.

[29] Very little has been written in Western languages on the declining legitimacy of the political clergy. This summary relies on the following indispensable sources: Farhad Khosrokhovar, *L'Utopie Sacrifiée: Sociologie de la Révolution Iranienne* (Paris: Presses de la Fondation Nationale des Sciences Politiques, 1993), pp. 263–89; and Edward Shirley, 'Exhausted Revolutionaries' (mimeograph).

[30] See Economist Intelligence Unit, *Iran Country Report*, Third Quarter 1994, pp. 9–10.

[31] See Michel Malinksy, 'L'Iran à la Croisée des Chemins', *Espaces Stratégiques*, no. 55, March 1992, p. 197.

[32] Fariba Adelkhah, 'La République entre Fauteuils et Tapis: La Société et la Pouvoir', in Adelkhah, François Bayart and Olivier Roy, *Thermidor en Iran* (Paris: Editions Complexe, 1993), p. 82.

[33] Leonard Helfgott, 'The Structural Foundations of the National Minority Problem in Revolutionary Iran', *Iranian Studies*, vol. 13, nos 1–4, 1980, pp. 195–214.

[34] See *Mideast Mirror*, 9 September 1994, pp. 19–22.

[35] Ayatollah Khomeini, *Islam and Government* (Berkeley, CA: Mizan Press, 1981), p. 302.

[36] See Laurent Lamote, 'Iran's Foreign Policy and Internal Crisis', in Patrick Clawson (ed.), *Iran's*

Strategic Intentions and Capabilities, Institute for National Security Studies, National Defense University (Washington DC: National Defense University, 1994); and Andrew Whittley, 'Minorities and the Stateless in Persian Gulf Politics', *Survival*, vol. 35, no. 4, Winter 1993–94, p. 34.

[37] Private communication, April 1994.

[38] For an extensive analysis of Iran's centre–periphery and Sunni problems, see *Al-Wasat*, no. 107, 14–20 February 1994, pp. 17–20.

[39] Pakistan's own Sunni–Shi'i sectarian strife, which intensified in early 1995, does not bode well for stability along the Iran–Pakistani border.

[40] *SWB*, ME/2077, 18 August 1994, p. MED/2.

[41] For example, in 1979–80 the regular army proved less than enthusiastic to fulfil its assigned role to put down a large Kurdish insurgency. The *Pasdaran*, in a display of ideological fervour, showed greater offensive spirit. Now, 16 years later, *Pasdaran* units are reportedly reluctant to engage Kurdish guerrillas in large-scale operations, preferring instead a stable but uneasy status quo.

[42] For a detailed and damning analysis of the MKO, see *Wall Street Journal*, 4 October 1994, p. A1, A12.

[43] For more detail, see 'Iran: Complete Regulations of the IRI Armed Forces', in *FBIS*-NES, 27 October 1994, pp. 18–19.

[44] This section on the Qazvin riots is based on a private communication, October 1994, and February 1995; and *International Herald Tribune*, 8–9 October 1994, p. 2.

Chapter II

[1] Cited in *The Independent*, 10 June 1994.

[2] *Xinhua News Agency*, 9 June 1994.

[3] For the little material that is available on this aspect of Iranian 'diplomacy', see *Washington Post*, 21 November 1993; *Gulf States Newsletter*, no. 493, 22 August 1994, pp. 2–4; *Time*, 31 May 1993, pp. 46–51, and 21 March 1994, pp. 51–55.

[4] For an excellent discussion of this point see, Fred Halliday, 'An Elusive Normalization: Western Europe and the Iranian Revolution', *Middle East Journal*, vol. 48, no. 2, Spring 1994.

[5] See the extensive interview with Mohammad Javad Larijani, a Foreign Ministry official, in *Resalat*, 25 December 1988, pp. 3 and 8.

[6] See *Gulf States Newsletter*, no. 376, 11 December 1989, p. 4.

[7] See Torsten Wohlert, *Iran: Die Pragmatist Republik Gottes?: Transformation im Zeichen des Krieges* (Frankfurt: Verlag fur Interkulterelle Kommunikation, 1993), pp. 136–37.

[8] Michael Rothenburg, 'Russian and Iran: A Continuing Security Relationship', Science Applications International Corporation (SAIC), Foreign Systems Research Centre, McLean, VA, Analytic Note, 8 May 1992, p. 1.

[9] Iraq's regenerative strength has evoked a great deal of admiration and fear in Iran. *Kayhan International*, 12 June 1994, p. 2; and conversations with Iranian analysts, Tehran, June 1993.

[10] *Tehran Times*, 20 May 1993, pp. 1 and 10.

[11] Interior Minister Ali Mohammed Besharati in *SWB*, ME/1937, 4

March 1994, p. MED/9.
[12] *SWB*, ME/2100, 14 September 1994, p. MED/7.
[13] *Tehran Times*, 3 March 1992, p. 1.
[14] Interview with Shaul Bakhash, Washington DC, April 1994.
[15] See Anthony Hyman, 'Power and Politics in Central Asia's New Republics', *Conflict Studies*, no. 273, Royal Institute for the Study of Conflict and Terrorism, London, August 1994, pp. 13–14.
[16] Amalia von Gent, 'Azerbaijan: Oil, Armenians, Russians and Refugees', *Swiss Review of World Affairs*, no. 2, February 1994, p. 24.
[17] See Dilip Hiro, 'The Question of Azerbaijan', *The Nation*, 14 September 1992, p. 242; *The Independent*, 13 June 1992; and *Moscow News Weekly*, no. 27, 1992.
[18] Foreign Minister Ali Akbar Velayati made this point bluntly in an interview with *Al-Majalla*, 13–19 June 1993, p. 41.
[19] Foreign Minister Velayati's opening speech at the Fourth Seminar on 'Prospects for Peace and Stability in the Persian Gulf and Oman Sea', sponsored by the Foreign Ministry Institute for Political and International Studies, Tehran, 26–28 June 1993.
[20] This term is adapted from David Armstrong, *Revolution and World Order: The Revolutionary State in International Society* (Oxford: Clarendon Press, 1993).
[21] Dr Sohrab Shahabi, 'Iran and the Global Economy', *Iran Focus*, February 1995, p. 14.
[22] The original formulation of the DCP came in a keynote address delivered by Dr Martin Indyk of the US National Security Council in mid-1993; see 'The Clinton Administration's Approach to the Middle East', The Soref Symposium, Washington Institute for Near East Policy, 18 May 1993.

Chapter III

[1] For a historical survey, see Jean Calmard, 'Les Reformes Militaires sous les Qajars (1794–1925)', in Yann Richard (ed.), *Entre L'Iran et L'Occident: Adaptation et Assimilation d'Idées et techniques Occidentales en Iran* (Paris: Fondation de la Maison des Sciences de l'Homme, 1989).
[2] See the interview with Deputy Foreign Minister Ali Mohammed Besharati, in *FBIS*-NES, 22 November 1989, pp. 47–48; and comments of Brigadier-General Jalali, in *FBIS*-NES, 22 September 1988, pp. 37–38. See also Rafsanjani's vow to rebuild Iran's 'defensive power', in *FBIS*-NES, 3 February 1992, pp. 46–47; and 'Bazsazi Niru'haye Musallah: Nokhostin Vazefeh' ('Rebuilding Our Armed Forces is a Priority'), *Saff*, no. 106, 1367.
[3] See Francis Tusa, 'Iran Begins Rebuilding Its Military With Eastern Bloc Weaponry', *Armed Forces Journal International*, September 1989, pp. 29–30; and *The Guardian*, 29 April 1989.
[4] See *Kayhan*, 28 September 1989, p. 18.
[5] In a 1983 interview with *SAFF*, Speaker of the *Majlis*, Rafsanjani, noted that the Air Force had played an important role in supporting Iran's ground forces at the front, defending Iran's territorial waters, and halting Iraqi armoured thrusts into Khuzistan. See 'Deedgahaye riyasat-e- majlis shura'i islami darbareh naqsh artesh' ('The Speaker of the *Majlis* Views the Role of the Military'), *SAFF*, no. 50, 1362, pp. 8–12, 18–19; see also,

'Goftegu ba farmandeh niru'i hava'i' ('Interview with the Commander of the Air Force'), *SAFF*, no. 98, 1366, p. 12.

[6] See *Ibid*.

[7] *FBIS*-NES, 18 November 1988, p. 49.

[8] See *Salam*, 28 July 1992, p. 3.

[9] *Financial Times*, 8 February 1993, p. 4.

[10] A number of French-built *Mirage* fighters were among the planes that fled to Iran. Since the Iranians are not familiar with the *Mirage*, they have not been integrated into the Iranian Air Force.

[11] *SWB* SU/1516, 20 October 1992, p. A1/3.

[12] 'Goftegu ba farmandeh taktiki niru'i darya'i' ('Interview with Operations Commander of the Naval Forces'), *SAFF*, no. 53, 1363 , pp. 64–68.

[13] *FBIS*-NES, 28 November 1989, p. 70.

[14] Quoted in Mohammed Ziarati, 'Iranian National Security Policy', *Middle East International*, 3 April 1992, p. 18.

[15] For a detailed analysis, see Michael Eisenstadt, 'Déjà Vu All Over Again? Iran's Military Build-Up', unpublished paper, March 1994, pp. 17–21.

[16] John Jordan, 'The Iranian Navy', *Jane's Defence Review*, vol. 5, no. 5, May 1992, p. 216; Irina Hetsch, 'Die Islamische Republik Iran im Konfliktfeld des Nahens und Mittleren Ostens-Aussen und Sicherheitspolitik wahren des letzten Golfkrise', *Asien, Afrika und Lateinamerika*, no. 19, 1991, p. 440.

[17] Anthony Cordesman, *Iran and Iraq: The Threat from the Northern Gulf* (Boulder, CO: Westview Press, 1994), pp. 411–12.

[18] See the statement of US Director of Naval Intelligence, Rear Admiral Thomas Brooks before the Seapower, Strategic, and Critical Materials Committee of the House Armed Services Committee, Washington DC, 7 March 1991, p. 68.

[19] On the *Kilos*, see 'Russian Subs in the Market Place', *Maritime Defence*, vol. 18, no. 4, May 1993, pp. 106–8.

[20] See Barbara Starr, 'Iranian Torpedo Firings Cause US Consternation', *Jane's Defence Weekly*, 7 January 1995, p. 3.

[21] See *Bayan*, 22 June–22 July 1990, pp. 16–17.

[22] See 'Artesh jumhuriyeh islami Iran dar mantaqeh dargoon Shiraz: gozareshe az chegunegi maneuvre zerehi va piadeh niru'iyeh zamini' ('Army of the Republic of Iran in the Shiraz Area: Report of Armoured and Infantry Manoeuvres'), *SAFF*, no. 126, 1369, pp. 10–12.

[23] For details see, Anoushiravan Ehteshami, 'Iran's Revolution: Fewer Ploughshares, More Swords', *Army and Defence Quarterly Journal*, vol. 20, no. 1, January 1990, pp. 41–49

[24] See Homa Omid, *Islam and the Post-Revolutionary State in Iran* (New York: St Martin's Press, 1994), pp. 157–67.

[25] *FBIS*-NES, 27 October 1988, p. 54.

[26] 'Ayn Muravi, 'Khvarmeyaneh dar astaneh yek "jang ballistk"' ('The Middle East on the Eve of a Ballistic Missile Era'), *SAFF*, no. 108, 1367.

[27] An Iranian defence official vividly described the impact of the last war of the cities on Tehran, discussion with author, June 1993.

[28] See John Reed 'Defence Exports– Current Concerns', *Jane's Special Brief*, Section 8-Iran, April 1993.

[29] *The Times*, 12 November 1993.
[30] *FBIS*-NES, 29 January 1991, p. 55.
[31] W. Seth Carus, 'Proliferation and Security in Southwest Asia', *Washington Quarterly*, v. 17, n. 2, Spring 1994, p. 134; and *FBIS*, JPRS Report: Proliferation Issues, Russian Federation Foreign Intelligence Service Report, 'A New Challenge After the Cold War: Proliferation of Weapons of Mass Destruction', 5 March 1993.
[32] Alvin Cottrell, 'Iran's Armed Forces under the Pahlavis', in George Lenczowski (ed.), *Iran under the Pahlavis* (Palo Alto, CA: Hoover Institution Press, 1978), p. 428.
[33] Quoted in K. R. Singh, *Iran: Quest for Security* (New Delhi: Vikas Publishers, 1979), pp. 329–30.
[34] *Ettela'at*, 3 April 1993, cited in *FBIS*-NES, 9 April 1993, pp. 44–45.
[35] 'Der Iran und die Bombe', *Osterreiche Militariche Zeitschrift*, March–April 1992, p. 165.
[36] See 'Novy Vyzov Posle "Kholodnoy Voyny": Raaprostraneniye Oruzhiya Massovogo Unichtozeniya' ('A New Challenge After the Cold War: Proliferation of Weapons of Mass Destruction'), in Joint Publications Research Service, *Nuclear Developments*, 5 March 1993, pp. 11–12.
[37] See 'Pakistan–Iran Nuclear Cooperation Revealed', *Defense and Foreign Affairs Weekly,* 21–27 November 1988, p. 2; and 'An Iran–Pakistan Link', *Foreign Report*, 17 December 1987.
[38] *Washington Post*, 12 April 1988, p. D2.
[39] For more details, see *Al Wasat*, no. 156, 23 January 1995, p. 11.
[40] See, Romedio Graf von Thun, Nordkorea und Iran: Streben nach Atomwaffen' ('North Korea and Iran: Quest for Atomic Weapons'), *Europäische Sicherheit*, November 1992, p. 605.
[41] *FBIS*-JPRF, 7 November 1991, p. 23; and *Washington Post*, 17 November 1992, p. A30.
[42] See *Technologies Underlying Weapons of Mass Destruction*, Office of Technology Assessment, Washington DC, pp. 31–34.
[43] See Seymour Hersh, 'The Wild East', *Atlantic Monthly*, June 1994.
[44] *Kayhan International*, 9 November 1991, p. 2; *Washington Post*, 17 November 1992, p. A30.
[45] 'Atomwaffen gehören nicht zu Unser Verteidungstrategie' ('Atomic Weapons Are Not Part of Our Defence Strategy'), *Deutsche Welle, Monitor Dienst Nahost*, 3 March 1993.
[46] See Udo Ulfkotte, 'Iran entwickelt keine Nuclearwaffen', ('Iran is Not Developing Nuclear Weapons'), *Frankfurter Allgemeine Zeitung*, 31 July 1992.
[47] *Tehran Times*, 24 February 1994, p. 1,14.
[48] *Kayhan International*, 9 November 1991, p. 2; *Washington Post*, 17 November 1992, p. A30.
[49] In early 1992, Rafsanjani stated: 'We seek nuclear technology for peaceful uses and consider this path to be right for all countries which have the potential to acquire it'. *FBIS*-NES, 12 February 1992, p. 55.
[50] Jalil Roshandel and Sa'ideh Lotfian, 'Is Iran a Nuclear-Capable State?', *Tehran Times*, 10 April 1993, p. 4.
[51] See *FBIS*-NES, 21 April 1993, pp. 44–45.
[52] David Fulghum, 'Mideast Nations Seek Counter to Air Power', *Aviation Week and Space Technology*, 7 June 1993, p. 77.

[53] See, for example, *New York Times*, 8 November 1992, p. 18; Richard Barnard and Barbara Opall, 'Israel Targets Iran Nuke Plans', *Defense News*, 4–10 July 1994, pp. 1 and 29; *Los Angeles Times*, 7 February 1995, p. 1, 16; and *FBIS-NES*, 6 September 1994, pp. 25–26.
[54] *Washington Post*, 13 March 1993.
[55] See, for example, 'Worry over a Nuclear Mideast', *Mideast Mirror*, 17 June 1992, pp. 7–9; and *Middle East International*, 26 June 1992, pp. 4–5.
[56] *Jumhuri-ye Islami*, 21 June 1992, p. 1, 19.

Conclusion

[1] See the extensive interview with Ata'ollah Mohajerani in *Al Majallah,* 6 November 1994, p. 30.
[2] Foreign Minister Ali Akbar Velayati has so far indicated that he is not interested in running for the presidency.
[3] David Remnick, *Lenin's Tomb* (London: Penguin Books, 1994), p. 533.
[4] Decentralisation is defined as the weakening of the authority of the central power, and not as the disintegration of Iran as a nation-state. The latter is unlikely.